Time and Tide

Book Nine of the
Coming Back to Cornwall series

Katharine E. Smith

HEDDON PUBLISHING

www.heddonpublishing.com
www.facebook.com/heddonpublishing
@PublishHeddon

Katharine E. Smith is a writer, editor and publisher.

An avid reader of contemporary writers such as Kate Atkinson, David Nicholls, Helen Dunmore and Anne Tyler, Katharine's aim is to write books she would enjoy reading – whether literary fiction or more light-hearted, contemporary fiction.

Time and Tide is her fourteenth novel and a continuation of this popular Coming Back to Cornwall series, which was originally intended to be a trilogy. Connections is Katharine's latest series, with book one (*Elise*) and book two (*Maggie*) available now, and book three well underway.

Katharine runs Heddon Publishing from her home in Shropshire, which she shares with her husband, their two children, and their border collie.

You can join Katharine's mailing list, get a free short story, and a free e-book of
Writing the Town Read,
by visiting Katharine's website:
www.katharineesmith.com.

For our amazing NHS

Time and Tide

Time to Celebrate

Our wonderful town is looking beautiful, decked out with colourful bunting, and fresh, cheerful hanging baskets outside shop doorways. There are posters on every wall, every lamp-post, in houses, shops, pubs, cafes... drumming up excitement for the upcoming festival day; a new celebration for the town and one that, it is hoped, will become an annual event.

Like everywhere else, the people of this town are in need of some cheering up, as we emerge from the last year or so, which has revolved around lockdowns, fear and anxiety. Daily briefings which at first seemed utterly unreal, and daily figures of infections, hospitalisations, and deaths. All of this, which would have seemed unthinkable just two years ago, has become the norm. It's been interesting to see how quickly we developed new habits, of social distancing, mask-wearing, and staying home, rarely seeing people outside immediate family, housemates or our 'bubbles'.

As the vaccination programme has started to take effect, like meerkats, we've begun to emerge, sticking our heads out of our burrows, checking to see if it really is safe to come out. Cautiously edging out into the world... but many of us are still on edge. Still nervous. Not really sure if we can trust what we are being told.

All those little things we used to take for granted: a meal in a restaurant; a coffee with a friend; a drink in a pub (bought by just walking in and going up to the bar – imagine!)... their value is revealed now that we have had to live without them.

And so it has been decided by the town council, and the Christmas lights committee, and the Christmas tree committee, and the Christmas fair committee… you get the picture… that, even though it is not Christmas, but the exact opposite end of the year, it is time for a celebration. There is funding sitting unused from the traditional winter celebration that was all but cancelled, and so plans are afoot for a midsummer celebration. A point in the year when the town has really come to life – but before the school summer holidays and the chaos that those weeks bring, with traffic-clogged roads and Fore Street rammed with holidaymakers. This celebration has been designed with the resident population at its heart. A treat for us all, and a way to bring people out once more. There are still many who don't feel safe, or who have lost their confidence during weeks and months of shielding and essentially seeing nobody.

And for the many of us still concerned with the safety aspects of bringing so many people together, town mayor Peter Oswald assures me that the utmost care has been taken to make sure that we remain as safe as can be. "There will be one-way systems, and limited numbers inside shops, cafes, etc, as per any normal day. Besides, it will be mid-June, and the majority of the fun will be outdoors. On our beautiful beaches and streets."

So make a date in your diaries. Saturday June 19th. The bunting is out, and the town is ready to welcome you.

1

"Annoying it's the day before the solstice retreat starts!" says Julie, skimming the newspaper article. "We're going to have to try and keep clear heads, so we can look all healthy and fresh when our guests arrive on the Sunday."

"I know. Very inconsiderate! But Lizzie says she can hold the fort here on the Sunday, if we're still recovering."

"Ha! Chance would be a fine thing. I'll probably just have a shandy or three."

"Yeah, that sounds about right for me as well." Those heady days of drinking and partying into the night are long gone, for both of us. They were even before the children came along, to be honest. Even so, I want to be able to enjoy the town's celebrations without worrying too much about work the next day. I'm grateful to Lizzie, for offering to take the strain if need be.

"Do you think Lizzie will come down to town for it? Even for a little while?" asks Julie.

"I doubt it. She'll enjoy having Amethi to herself, after everyone's cleared off in the morning. I think she misses those lockdown days."

"I don't blame her. Think how busy town's going to be. All those people! Urgh!" Julie grins.

"I know. Think of the germs." We are only half-joking. As the article intimated, the last year or so has been all about germs, and trying to avoid them. Most of the world has been swept by a wave of coronavirus, Covid-19. A virus which has ranged from being unnoticeable to some, to a horrible flu-like illness which in some cases has had long-lasting effects on general health, to intensive care and even death for millions of others, worldwide. Since March of last year, we have had to get used to long periods of being confined to our homes and gardens. For a while we were allowed out just once a day for exercise, and never with anyone outside our own household. It's been unbelievable, or at first it seemed that way, but, also as the article says, it is amazing how quickly those things came to seem normal. Keeping two metres' distance from another human being became the norm. Bumping elbows in greeting, instead of a hug or a handshake. Wearing face masks indoors, and even outdoors. Applying hand gel a hundred times a day. Washing hands for as long as it took to sing two renditions of Happy Birthday. Who could possibly have imagined all this, just two years ago?

It has felt like any other human was a cause for suspicion. If anyone near you so much as coughed, or cleared their throat, you would step surreptitiously away. It has, in short, been horrible. And all the more so for people who were already lonely, and isolated. And for people stuck in a home with no outdoor space. The power of human touch has never felt so vital, and when we were allowed to hug again (yes, we had to be told when we would be allowed to do this), it seemed like an incredible luxury. Unless you're one of those people who hates hugs, and at pains to conserve personal space. If you're one of those people, the pandemic probably had its upside.

Lizzie is not one for crowds – and wasn't, even before covid struck. I did worry about her being quite so alone during the worst parts of the lockdowns. The guy she's been seeing, Med, was in France, with his ex and his kids, which must have been hard. "Not really," Lizzie had said when I'd suggested this to her, "he needs to be with his kids, and I need to be here."

She's one of a kind. I established that years ago, and maybe out of all of us, Lizzie has been affected the least by all the goings-on. The main change for her was coming to live at Amethi, in the cottage where I once lived alone, before Sam and Sophie came to join me – then where Jonathan and Janie lived, before they went to Spain. It is also the place where I gave birth to Holly – greatly supported by Lizzie.

Letting her move in there has been the least that we could do. I know I used to feel a little bit out on a limb, when I lived there alone, but for Lizzie I suspect that many of the best times have been while we've not been able to have any guests, and she has had the place to herself. The Mowhay – the communal space where we hold parties, and yoga courses, and writing workshops – has been her own personal yoga studio, and she's had the fields and woods and wildlife to connect with. She reluctantly allowed herself to become part of Sam's and my 'bubble' when this idea was introduced, as a way to end isolation for people living alone. But she rarely took advantage of the new freedom to spend time with other people.

The kids love her, though. Poor little Holly, who was just three months old when the first national lockdown was enforced, has had very little contact with people outside of our four walls. During our family walks, we would pass by the Sail Loft and wave to Mum and Dad. Ben loved this, although he was also devastated every time, as he wanted to go in, and to run and cuddle Mum and Dad, and was very frustrated that this was just not allowed. It was hard enough for us adults to get our heads around it all, and to miss out on social and physical contact with the people we love… so what was it like for the kids? I suspect that it will be some time yet before we really know how they've been affected.

We'd sometimes pass by Karen and Ron's place on our walks as well, but a little less frequently as time went on, because they weren't as convinced by the whole social distancing thing as we were. They'd encourage Ben to come for a hug, and Karen would ask for a cuddle with Holly, and it all became quite difficult and awkward, really. I felt awful not seeing them, and I know they found it really hard. Sam was adamant about it, though; more than me, really.

"If they haven't seen anyone else, though, it should be OK," I'd suggest.

"But how do we know they haven't seen anyone else? And also, what are we teaching the kids? That it's OK to bend the rules for our own benefit? And what if they pick up the virus and pass it on, and we pass it on to your mum and dad – or anyone else, for that matter?"

That was the clincher for me. Mum was very ill in hospital not so many years ago, and both she and Dad are in their seventies. Young and sprightly, for the most part, but it wasn't worth the risk. There was no telling how the virus might affect somebody and there has been a lot of emphasis on its greater effect on older people, or those with underlying health conditions.

Anyway, over her first year-and-a-half, Holly has had nowhere near as many socialising opportunities as Ben did at her age. So when Lizzie did pop round, or if we went up to see her at Amethi, it has been great for my little girl. Lizzie does seem to have a special attachment to her, and it appears that the feeling is mutual. When Holly was smaller, the moment she saw Lizzie, she'd fling her arms in the air, and rock back and forth, trying to propel herself forwards for a cuddle. Lizzie would tentatively pick her up, always wary of passing on any germs, although she was probably the safest of us all, keeping all contact with other humans to the absolute minimum. She was making full use of the vegetable garden at Amethi, and had arrangements with local farmers for them to drop off waxed-paper-wrapped cheeses, and bottles of unpasteurised milk. She's also become pretty expert at making sour dough bread, and I'm always happy when she comes to visit with a warm loaf wrapped in a tea towel. These days, Holly can run up to her, and Lizzie will sweep her into the air, laughing.

I think she appreciates being able to spend time with us when it suits her, but I also think Julie is right that Lizzie is probably not too worried about missing out on the town's festivities, whereas I would be gutted if we couldn't go.

"I wish I had a lead for Zinnie, though," Julie sighed. "Imagine losing her in a crowd."

Zinnia, initially slow to begin walking, is now an absolute tearaway. She's a little bit younger than Ben and, although not Julie's biological daughter, she is every inch the determined, free spirit that her mum is.

I laugh. "Don't! And you know what it's like in town. She wouldn't get far, even if she did make a dash for it.

Somebody would see her, and catch her."

"Yeah, like Dave at the post office the other day," Julie says, grimacing. "I was in line, holding her hand, and she was being good as gold. Then when it was my turn to pay, she legged it, and she'd have been out of the door if he hadn't caught her. She was *not* happy."

Luckily, Julie being Julie, she sees the funny side of this. If Holly or Ben were to put me through anything like that, I don't think I'd be quite as relaxed. I love being a parent, but I feel the weight of responsibility quite heavily. Which is not to say Julie is not responsible; she just finds it easier than I do to go with the flow. She always has.

"You could try reins," I say.

"Are you kidding!" Julie splutters. "It'd be like the Tasmanian Devil. She'd be gnawing at my arm to get away."

"Well, we'll stick together, and hopefully she'll be happy hanging out with Ben."

"Yep, having him there will definitely help."

"And hopefully the weather's going to be good."

"Imagine… wall-to-wall sunshine. Light till about half ten. Live music at the harbour. A beer outside the Mainbrace…"

"The fairground at the rugby club…"

"Yeah, well, I'll probably try to keep any time there to a minimum. Fairgrounds are the worst place for fighting. Think how many times there were fights when the fair came to town back home."

"You're right. It's weird, isn't it? They're supposed to be fun; the name stipulates that. But also, this is home now, Julie. You belong to Cornwall. Don't forget it."

"As if I could."

The office phone begins to ring and Julie answers with a

friendly, "Amethi, can I help you?"

I'm still getting used to us being back up here and working together. We had to 'mothball' the business for quite a while last year, but nevertheless it seemed there was always something to do. Julie and I would work on our laptops at home and catch up via phone, Zoom, WhatsApp messages, as and when required and families allowed. The office space is small here, so it is quite strange, being in this little room with somebody outside my immediate family. But once we started to welcome guests back, we decided it was time to bite the bullet, and that we couldn't really manage from home. Julie certainly couldn't, what with her being the chef… But even for me, though a lot of my work is management and admin-based, it makes so much more sense to be on site. And I like it, to be honest. I missed it. I missed the distinction between work and home, I missed the contact with Julie, and I just missed being at Amethi.

It's really been a tough time, and yet we've been fortunate to have not even been touched by the virus itself. I can't begin to imagine what it's been like for those who have. Some fun and light-heartedness is very much needed, and I can't wait for June 19th. I know it's only a small thing, really; a festival in our little town, but I am looking forward to it so much, and I know I'm not the only one.

2

First things, first, though: wedding dress-shopping with Karen. Despite any differences of opinion over the safety (or otherwise) of lockdown behaviour, and adherence to rules, Sam and I are both really pleased that she has found Ron. He's a lovely man, and seems to have a genuinely stabilising influence on Karen.

"I just don't think Mum has ever really been happy before," Sam said after we'd been for a walk with them along the coastal path – Holly secured to Sam in a baby backpack, and Ben's hand firmly held in Ron's.

I had walked along behind them, holding Meg on her lead, and smiling at the sight before me. Up ahead, Ben was listening keenly to Ron, who was no doubt dishing out pearls of wisdom about the sea, and safety – "You're never too young to start learning," Ron says, and I don't disagree. Then there was Sam, walking along and chatting with his mum, Holly's sun-hatted head lolling against him as she drifted off.

Just the act of Sam chatting to his mum is a thing to behold. It has taken him a long time – more than twenty years – to get over her abandoning him at the tender age of sixteen. Of course, she doesn't see it like that (or claims she doesn't): "I was out at work at sixteen, and I barely saw my mum or dad. I don't think I much wanted to, in all honesty!

It's a good age to learn to stand on your own two feet," she will say, I sometimes think a little defensively.

I am sure she thinks my upbringing was far too sheltered. An only child, with a university education, supported by my parents. I did have a part-time job at Pizza Hut when I was in sixth form, but to be honest anything I earned I spent on nights out, or clothes, magazines, CDs, etc. I had a summer in Cornwall aged eighteen, which was when I first met Sam, and the first time I'd been away from Mum and Dad, aside from sleepovers and the occasional school trip. By that time, Sam had been supporting himself for two years, and sharing a flat with a friend. He says he didn't mind at first, as the independence was exciting, but the novelty soon wore off, and he was lonely and living off rice and pot noodles a lot of the time.

I sometimes try to imagine Ben and Holly being sixteen. It seems impossible that in just over ten years, Ben will be the same age that Sam was when his mum left for Spain.

"What do you think?" Karen says, stepping out of the changing room.

She is in a peacock-blue dress, with a puffed-out knee-length skirt, and plenty of cleavage showing.

"It's…" I say, but she has already decided what my answer will be.

"Not weddingy enough, is it? Maybe it'll do for my going-away outfit."

"Are you having one of those?" I ask. As far as I am aware, she and Ron aren't actually going away. The rules keep changing about where people are allowed to travel to, so they have opted for a couple of nights at the Bay Hotel in town, with a view to a 'proper' honeymoon when they know that they can go abroad without the risk of their holiday being cancelled, or having to rush back halfway through their time away because the country they're staying in has been returned to the red list.

"Of course!" Karen says now, like it's obvious. "I want to do it properly. Never been married before, have I? I remember my friends getting married off, one by one, and watching them leave their wedding receptions in their smart new suits, with smart new luggage to match. I always wanted Gareth to ask me, but by the time I was pregnant with Sam, I knew there was no chance. He didn't do a runner straight away, to give him his due, but he was as much use as a chocolate teapot, to me and to Sam. Best thing he did, when he did finally leave us. Course, we had Janie by then as well."

She is turning around in front of the mirror while she says all this, admiring herself from every angle. To be honest, she looks pretty great. The dress is not something I would wear, but that's neither here nor there. Karen is a good ten years younger than my mum, and seems even younger in some ways. They are so different, and yet they get on really well these days. So well, in fact, that Mum has come with us today, because Karen has asked her to be maid of honour.

"Really?" Mum had asked, genuinely surprised and delighted. "I never expected to be asked to do something like that at this time of my life! I would love to, Karen, if you're sure."

"Of course I'm sure!" Karen said, hugging Mum. "And Sophie and Janie can be my bridesmaids."

I had stood by, already realising there wouldn't be such a role for me in this wedding. But I really didn't mind. And I was just as delighted as Mum that Karen had asked her to be maid of honour. Ever since I moved back down to Cornwall, I've felt this increasing kind of warmth, as my world and the people in it have come together, creating an extended family. It's like a well-woven basket, with everyone somehow fitting together, and keeping each other strong.

"What do you think, Sue?" Karen asks Mum now.

"We-e-ell… goddammit, you look stunning, Karen! I wouldn't waste that dress on a going-away outfit. You'll be a knock-out bride in it!"

"You don't think I should tone it down. Maybe ivory, or white?"

"I think that ship's sailed, Karen!" Mum says, and they both laugh, while I think I would never be able to get away with being that cheeky to my mother-in-law.

I think the turning point in their relationship came when we were allowed to go out for exercise with somebody from outside our own households or bubbles. Sometimes I would walk with Mum, but sometimes she'd already have arranged to go with Karen. Clearly the walking had turned to talking, and they'd found some real common ground somewhere.

"Well what about you, Sue? And the bridesmaids?"

"How about dark green, or dark blue?" I suggest, keen to stay involved, and also bearing in mind my promise to Janie, that I will make sure Karen chooses something she'll like.

Far away in Spain, none of us have seen Janie, or Jonathan, since way before the pandemic began. Janie has agreed to come across for Karen's hen do, and then stay till the wedding a couple of weeks later. She is keen to keep travelling to a minimum because, while perhaps, just perhaps, the worst of this virus is over, we are not out of the woods yet. Karen thinks this is ridiculous, of course, and has given Janie a hard time over it, wanting her to come dress shopping with us, and even offering to pay her way over. But Janie is standing her ground. Which is a lot easier to do via Zoom than it is face-to-face.

"Sorry, Mum, but I don't want to be flying back and forth like that when there's a pandemic on. I'll be there for the hen do, and Jon can come over in time for the wedding."

I'm sure she somehow manages to make the connection fail, when she's had enough. She's an IT expert, and I wouldn't put it past her. Jonathan, meanwhile, stays safely in the background, making himself busy in the kitchen, or just passing through on his way out to work at the Michelin-starred restaurant where he's managed to land himself a role.

In the changing room, Karen considers my colour choices. "Hmmm…" She is perhaps thinking more along the lines of neon-pink or lime-green.

"Oh yes, either of Alice's suggestions would work well, and create a perfect background, for your brighter blue," says Mum. "After all, we don't want the bride to be upstaged, do we?" I am sure Janie will be grateful for this interjection, though I am quite sure Mum has her own interests at heart as well.

"Well, if you think so…" Karen doesn't look convinced.

"You look stunning!" one of the ladies from the shop appears through the curtain at the perfect time. "Are you decided, or do you want to try more?" To be fair to this lady, we have been there for nearly an hour, and she's been back and forth with a good ten or twelve dresses so far.

"Karen?" Mum looks at her, and raises her eyebrows.

"I'll take it!" Karen exclaims, and we all smile (and perhaps breathe a sigh of relief).

"And the bridesmaid dresses…?" the woman asks hopefully.

"I know the perfect ones," I say, "but I think we all need a break. How about we buy your dress, Karen, and then go and get some lunch somewhere? What do you say?"

"I say great idea, love," says Mum, and Karen has little choice but to agree. Besides, now her dress has been selected, I feel like she's losing interest, and I hope that over lunch, Mum and I can work on her to let us choose the other dresses – with her having final say, of course. Perhaps I'll treat her to a glass of prosecco, to help seal the deal.

3

After a long day shopping (in fact, the prosecco only hardened Karen's resolve to choose *all* the dresses for the wedding, and buy them all today, so we spent another two or three hours traversing the shopping centre until we could all agree on something), all I want to do is have tea with Sam and the kids, put my pyjamas on, and lie on the settee. However, tonight is the monthly business network group meeting and I promised Julie I would go to this one. So my lazy night in is not to be.

Tomorrow, I tell myself. *Tomorrow.*

Probably.

The meeting is being hosted on the huge outside deck of the Bay Hotel – this way, the number of attendees does not have to be limited in the same way. When it was first opening, I had fears that the Bay would be encroaching on Amethi's ground, but it is far more glamorous than what Julie and I have to offer. Lydia, who a long time ago was a waitress at the Sail Loft, is doing a fantastic job of managing it, and it's booked up a year in advance. Her boss Felicity is currently somewhere overseas with her rich new boyfriend, and Lydia couldn't be happier.

"It's so nice just to get on with work and not have to worry about her breathing down my neck! And we're doing very nicely, so she's not worried. I think now she can see that we're making a profit and building a great reputation, she might not feel the need to stick her nose into everything. Fingers crossed, anyway."

Lydia is currently officially single, but being actively pursued by a very up-and-coming and popular young actor by the name of Si Davey. I can tell she likes him, but she's keeping her cards close to her chest. He's a regular visitor these days, staying at the Bay Hotel every couple of months if he can; ostensibly to retreat from London and film sets, and the media (though they are never too far behind), but I know that he and Lydia do spend some time together. However, she's maintaining a professional distance, or so she says.

"Come on, Lydia!" I have pushed her, laughingly. "It's Si Davey. Si Davey! Don't tell me you're not interested."

"He's a hotel guest, and I'm the manager," she will reply primly, but with a hint of a smile.

"And that's all there is to it, I suppose."

"Exactly," she will say, pressing her lips together in a way that suggests she's hiding something.

"Have it your way."

Tonight, Lydia is welcoming all of the meeting attendees personally. I'm sure if Felicity could see the hotch-potch of people sitting amongst her beautifully kept raised beds, and water features, she'd go pale. The tables have been arranged in such a way that there is a space for the speakers to stand, but unfortunately for them, they also have to compete with the attention-grabbing, sparkling sea beyond. So they'd better keep things interesting.

There are so many local business owners here, from Paul

Waters (my long-ago date and local millionaire businessman) with his wife, Shona, who is also an extremely successful businesswoman with her own PR firm – of whom Felicity would certainly approve – to a few of the pleasure-boat owners, and Shelagh from the butchers on one of the side streets, to whom I suspect Felicity would be less welcoming.

I help myself to a coffee, and go to sit with Shona. I say with Shona, but I try to stay at least a metre away from her, across the other side of the table. It's so unnatural, all this social distancing.

"Hi, Alice! Great to see you." Her soft Scottish accent is warm as ever. "Looks like a busy night!"

"Well, there aren't many options for a night out at the moment!" I smile. "But actually, the pandemic seems to have knocked us all closer together. We've all been affected by it, and I think we might be able to help each other. Plus, everybody wants to be involved in the festival. It will be good for us all – as businesses, and just as people."

"It does seem like a big deal."

"It really is. And I know it seems a bit mean, having it before most of the tourists are here, but I think it's important that we all get to enjoy it, to celebrate the fact we've got through the hardest time – I hope. You know what it gets like in high season, too. Town will be heaving."

"I totally get it. And I've offered to do some PR, too. Not that this town needs any more!"

"No – if anything, we could do with a few less visitors! But saying that in the tourism trade is like blasphemy."

"Aye, well I won't quote you on that," she smiles.

Paul, on her other side, is busy chatting with a man who is from the fishing fleet of old. He now works in a small family business called Cornish Spliced, along with his daughters and granddaughter – repurposing old fishing ropes to make dog leads, dog toys, and the like. I often see them down on the beaches, searching for suitable material. I love the idea of such a family concern, and imagine Ben and Holly becoming involved in Amethi one day. No doubt they'll want to do the exact opposite, though, and maybe even get as far away from here as they possibly can. The thought makes my stomach churn, but hopefully when they're older I'll find it easier to accept that they have to live their lives as they choose.

Paul turns now and smiles at me. I try not to think of how much I used to find that smile attractive… but it is different now. He's undeniably gorgeous, but I think I can just accept that as part of him, without it swaying me either way. Our relationship never really got off the ground, and that was the right thing. I still fantasize about staying over at his house, but these days it's more about the amazing views and the beach at the bottom of his garden than anything else.

"How are you, Alice? Great turnout, eh?"

"Yes, amazing! Who's that, just coming in? I haven't seen him before."

At events like this, I realise how much I have settled into life here, that I recognise every face, even if I don't know everyone personally. However, the man walking in now is not somebody I've seen before. I would definitely remember him. He is quite a large man, and is doing nothing to hide it. He's kitted out in a loud Hawaiian-style shirt and mustard-coloured trousers that look like something Michael Portillo would be proud to wear. The man has a big, open smile on his face, outlined by a short, neat, dark beard, and he takes a seat heavily on the same bench as Diane Norris, who has a hairdressing salon down in the heart of town. She is quite petite, Diane, and I could almost picture her being catapulted into the air when the man sits down. Instead, I see her politely shuffle along ever-so-slightly, hoping he won't notice. But apparently, he does, and he laughs loudly, and offers his elbow to bump, in the strange new covid-safe way of greeting. She politely raises her elbow to his.

Lydia brings the gathering to order. "Good evening, everybody! It's wonderful to see so many of you here tonight, if a little unexpected!" There is a ripple of laughter. Many people here will have known Lydia as she's grown up in the town – as a teenager, she was a pillar for her parents, and helped take care of her little brothers, whilst simultaneously studying and working as a waitress at the Sail Loft Hotel. I can't think of anybody who would not want to see her doing well for herself.

"So it's a bit harder to do the usual one-minute introductions," she continues, "and besides, I think we can assume most of you know each other. Instead, I think it might be best if we ask any new business owners to introduce themselves, and then we can focus on the festival, and how we as the business community can support it. How does that sound?"

"Perfect!" shouts a voice from the back.

"Thank you," Lydia smiles.

"Will Si be coming to the festival?" another voice pipes up. Lydia flushes slightly. This is one of the downsides of life in a small town. It is very, very, hard to keep anything secret.

"I'll start!" the large man stands up, saving Lydia from further embarrassment, whether intentionally or not.

"Thank you, Mr…?" Lydia smiles graciously, possibly gratefully, at him as he stands.

"Just call me Craig. Crazy Craig," he says, turning and smiling benignly around. "Proprietor of Crazy Craig's Castles…" he expounds. His accent is immediately familiar to me, sounding not too different from my dad's. A fellow Midlander! Funny how, even though I feel so at home here in Cornwall, I still have an unwavering sense of familiarity and belonging when it comes to the West Midlands. It makes me a little nostalgic – not homesick, exactly, but I suppose my roots are there, and nothing can change that.

"Bouncy castles!" Craig's voice booms through the speakers. "Oh, sorry, I think I was holding the mike a bit close! I'm Craig Cash, and I come from Birmingham, or near enough, if you couldn't guess. I've just started my new business down here in Cornwall. Maybe I should call it Craig's Cornish Castles," he suggests genially.

"You're not Cornish, though, are you?" somebody heckles. I can't see who it was. The meeting definitely has a different feel to the usual ones. It's more like one of the town council meetings, which I was shocked to see are almost always standing-room only.

"No, you're right," Craig smiles good-naturedly. "I'll stick to Crazy Craig, then."

"You do that, mate." I see who it is this time. Nick, one of the guys Sam used to go to school with.

"We've already got bouncy castles!" somebody else calls. "Take 'em back home with you."

"And don't forget to shut the door on your way out."

"That would be a bit difficult, being as we're outside," Craig smiles genially. To his credit, he doesn't look moved either way by the heckles. "Always room for more bouncy castles, eh? Kids can't get enough of 'em. Adults, too. I'm not here to step on anyone's toes, though. Or bounce on them!"

"Thank you, Craig," Lydia moves easily towards him, and slides the microphone out of his hand. "And I'm sure we all wish you well. There is a lovely community here, not just on the business side of things, and if you need anything, I'm sure there will be plenty of people happy to help. Do you have a website and contact details for your new business?"

"Just getting it all sorted," Craig smiles, turns and walks back to his seat. Diane smiles at him when he sits, but I am not sure he notices. When he sits down, he clasps his hands together, as if to prevent them from shaking. He is perhaps not as thick-skinned as he'd like to appear.

Peter, the town mayor, steps in, and talk turns to the upcoming festival. Despite the ribbing of poor old Craig, there really is a lot of genuine generosity in this town. The pubs, restaurants, cafes and shops are all working together, to coordinate a united look and feel to the main streets. There is a huge raffle being organised, with almost everybody here donating a prize. Julie has authorised me to offer a personalised menu cooked by her, and delivered by me to the lucky winner's home. There are bouquets of flowers; surf lessons; pub meals; a beautiful painting by a local artist; fudge; a cream tea for two; a spa break at the Bay Hotel… the list seems endless. Craig offers an afternoon's bouncy castle hire, which is very nice of him, given the welcome he's received. But also, I think, quite an astute way to start himself off with a good reputation in the town.

At the 'comfort break', I make a point of finding him, to introduce myself. He is a tall man, which helps him carry his bulk, and I feel quite small next to him, like I need to tug on his sleeve to get his attention.

"Your accent sounds like home!" I say.

"You a Brummie girl?" he asks with interest.

"Well, near enough! You'll have to meet my dad, he and my mum run the Sail Loft Hotel. They're not here tonight. Still trying to avoid crowded places."

"Yeah, well, I can't say I blame them. I have to be honest, I thought twice about coming here, but I've had my two jabs, and I needed to show my face."

"I hope you didn't mind the heckles."

"What, that? I've heard much worse, I can tell you! No, water off a duck's back, bab."

"That's alright then. Well, I'm Alice and I run a little place called Amethi, just outside town, with my business partner, Julie. She's from up your way, as well! We moved down here together, and both live in town now. And we've both got kids, so I've got a feeling we'll be bumping into each other at parties and school fetes!"

"I hope so. I know there must be other established businesses doing what I do. I really don't want to tread on anybody's toes, like I said. I just wanted, well I dreamed about, moving here for a long time, and then I came into some money, and I thought after the miserable year we've just had, what do people want? Some fun, that's what. And what's more fun than a bouncy castle?"

"I'm sure you'll settle in, Craig. I love it down here. I've never looked back. Though it is nice to hear your accent! I'd better get going now, though… I'm going to slip away

23

before the meeting resumes, don't tell anyone!" My tiredness has caught up with me, and I need to go home. Sometimes these meetings can run and run, and I don't have the energy tonight. "It's lovely to meet you. And I hope your business goes really well. It might take a while… I'm sure you already know that."

"I've planned for it," he says. "I'm in it for the long-haul. And I do want to make some cash, but I really do want to make sure people have some fun again."

"Then I think you will do really well," I smile. "I'll look forward to seeing you at another meeting, if not before."

"Thanks, Alice," he smiles.

I say bye to Paul and Shona, and Lydia, and a variety of other people, on my way out, but I try to keep my head down, and keep on going. It would be all too easy to be drawn into any number of conversations, and not get away for another hour or more.

But before I head back, I take a few moments to walk up past the hotel, leaning on the railings and looking out across the sea. I hear a smattering of applause from the meeting and feel a twinge of guilt for leaving early. But no, it's OK, I tell myself. I breathe in slow and steady, watching the late evening sunlight spill onto the iridescent waters. I could just run down to the beach, dash into the waves. Just briefly. But I'm in smart clothes. And I'm tired. And I wish I wasn't so old and boring.

Tomorrow, I tell myself. Before that quiet evening I've planned, I will come for a swim. *Promises, promises*, I think. But I will do my best to keep them both.

4

As it happens, I can only keep one of those promises. The quiet evening in gives way to an outing to the beach. It's been a long, hot day in the office, and Sam has also been stuck indoors at work, which he considers a necessary evil. His job at a conservation charity often allows him to be out and about around Cornwall: on the beaches; up on the moors; wading through the rivers and streams. This is why he has an all-year-round healthy glow, and barely an ounce of fat on him, despite approaching middle age.

"Approaching?" he had laughed, when I voiced this thought. "I think we've already arrived, Alice, I'm sorry to tell you."

"Well, you might have, but we're not even forty yet. And I'm planning to live till I'm at least 120, so actually I'm only a third of the way in. Middle age is a long way off."

"Whatever you say," he'd smiled and kissed me. "But if you're going for 120, then I'll try and do the same."

"Perfect." I had kissed him back.

I admire Sam now, in his board shorts and t-shirt, crouching to help Holly build a sandcastle. It's pointless, as Ben has already ascertained; he has taken his bucket and spade, and Ron, and gone a little way off, where he can build his fortress without his little sister crawling and jumping over it, and pushing handfuls of it into her mouth.

Luckily, Sam is more patient. With the sun gradually lowering in the sky beyond him, there is a faint outline around my husband; a glow, in fact. He is laughing as Holly pats the small pile of sand so hard that it collapses. She laughs, too, and does the same thing again, looking to him for approval. Moments like these just catch me sometimes, and I feel my heart swelling with love and at how very lucky I am.

"He's very good, doing all this after a hard day at work," Karen's voice intrudes on my thoughts.

My immediate reaction is that this is a dig at me. I often think Karen is of the opinion that what I do isn't work as such. It needles me, but she's never outright said as much, and I do realise it might be me being over-sensitive.

I fight the urge to say that I've had a hard day at work as well and instead, I agree. "He is. He's a brilliant dad."

"God knows he didn't have much of a role model," Karen sighs, and I feel myself soften towards her once more. It seems like her upcoming wedding has got her opening up about things she's always kept close to her chest before. I wonder what it was like for her, when Sam and Janie were little. There is more of an age gap between them than there is between my two, and Gareth left while Janie was a little baby – but from what Sam and Karen say, I gather he wasn't all that much use when he was around, anyway. And they didn't have a lot of money, but much of what they did have was often spent on his drink. Not a great life, for a young family – and now I'm a mum myself, I think I can begin to imagine how lonely she must have been. To me, there is no excuse for her up and going when Sam was so young, but maybe she had been bursting to change her life for such a long time, and when the idea took hold, she couldn't fight it. And perhaps to her mind, Sam really was old enough to look after himself.

Karen is a person with a strong drive to enjoy life, and she must have felt stifled for a long time, by such a useless, selfish partner, and two young children – and not a lot of money, or much in her life that was just for her. She worked here and there, but nothing ever seemed to stick. I imagine she could have been quite depressed. Maybe that drive to seek fun somehow found its way back, pushing its head up like a green shoot through the earth. Once focused on the sun, with no choice but to keep going. Not an excuse, perhaps, but a reason.

I lay my hand on her arm, her skin warm from the sun. Even though it's way past six, the heat of the day is still very much present. "You don't fancy a swim, do you? To cool down?"

"I do not!" she laughs. "But don't let me stop you. Go on, you work hard, too. Take this time while you can."

So she does think I work hard, after all. I smile, and hug her, to her apparent surprise and pleasure. "Thank you, Karen."

I stand, and pull my dress over my head. Without a thought for my wobbling, stretch-marked belly, and almost equally wobbly thighs (well, maybe one or two thoughts, if I'm honest), I tell Sam I'm going in, and I jog down the beach, straight into the cold, inviting water. I slow as the waves meet my knees, and I wade in, enjoying the deep, solid sound of each stride.

Children and parents are enjoying the shallows, and trying to catch the very gentle waves on their body boards, while further out a pair of older women swim side-by-side, not talking, but seemingly quite content. I push myself in past waist-depth, then plunge forwards so my shoulders and head are submerged. Back to the surface, gasping with pleasure, the sun and the saltwater making me blink. I forge ahead, until I'm swimming in the opposite direction to the two women, in a line parallel to the beach. To my right, I can just make out Ben with Ron, and Sam and Holly. Karen, I suspect, is taking the chance to lie back and catch the last of the day's rays.

I practise my front crawl, which I'm getting better at, and less self-conscious of. It's such a calm evening, and the sea is so placid tonight, the waves are barely noticeable as they roll gently by, politely making their way to shore. I turn and head back the way I came and then, when I am in line with my family, I tread water for a time, just taking it all in. The beach is busy, but in the best way. I love to see people enjoying themselves down here, whether they're local or visiting.

During the first lockdown, the beaches were so very, very different. Unnecessary travel had been banned. There were no tourists, and many down here were glad of it. Despite the impact on businesses, it was a once-in-a-lifetime opportunity to enjoy the place almost untouched. With people (other than essential frontline workers) told to stay at home to save lives, schools, 'non-essential' shops and other businesses were closed. Beaches were more-or-less empty, and any other people you might pass on your daily walk tended to stay a distance away, though there would often be a friendly wave from a distance. We felt quite safe down here, I think. Right out on a limb from the rest of the country, and the proportion of holiday homes to residential properties was more than apparent. It was indeed a little bit like a ghost town here... but the peace, and tranquillity! There was the bare minimum of traffic, and barely any pedestrians. The weather was incredible, too. From almost the moment that lockdown began, there was sunshine all day, every day. We spent so much time in the garden, or in the house with the French doors open. Meg was beside herself to have people to play with, or lie on, or be stroked by, whenever she liked.

Up where we live, it is mostly residential – lots of other young families, in fact – so the majority of sounds we might hear each day would be the steady boings of a trampoline; a football being kicked against a wall; a lawnmower engine; laughing and shrieking (and occasionally shouting and crying). I suppose we were lucky that our children were so young. They weren't missing out on school, although they were missing out on social experiences, but they had time with us that they might never have had otherwise – and vice versa. And while I would never, ever have wanted this awful thing to have happened to the world, like with most bad things, there were some positives, and Sam and I and Ben and Holly (and Meg) were some of the lucky ones to benefit.

I picture the beach as it was back then, with literally a handful of people on it. Nobody would have been allowed to stop for a picnic, or even stop at all. It was literally a case of passing through, on a walk or a run.

As restrictions eased, however, into the summer, it was a different matter. Always a popular holiday destination, once people were allowed to travel again (but not abroad), we were hit by what felt like a tidal wave of people. Amethi had been fully booked for the summer anyway, and we were able to honour those bookings, and glad – so very glad – to be outside the town. So were our guests. For the streets of the town were mayhem, and there was often very little respect for social distancing and the one-way systems that had been put in place to try and ensure everyone's safety.

People had been stuck at home for so long, and the whole country was ready for the chance to get moving again, and enjoy themselves. But with it came a kind of madness – and disregard. There was horrendous littering, heavy drinking, and anti-social behaviour – aggression and fights, and even attacks on gulls; many things that summer were much worse than in a normal year.

There is only one major hospital in Cornwall, and there were huge fears that it would be overwhelmed if the virus took hold here. When the population swelled to its peak, it was very stressful, and scary for the older folk, and anybody else deemed at more risk of serious illness. Also during that time, unemployment was on the rise, and the number of people claiming benefits rose dramatically, almost doubling during the nine months from the start of the lockdown to the end of the year. Businesses folded and crumbled, and there was a lot of bitterness, understandably.

Which is why this year is so important. A chance to get back some of that balance. And while I will never forget those quiet times, and in some ways would love to experience them again, they were for a good reason. And I know all over the country – all over the world – there were people putting themselves out there, risking their physical health and their mental health in trying to look after others, and keep things running, which sheds a slightly different light on the seemingly halcyon days.

I shake my head free of these thoughts. It doesn't do to dwell too much on all that we've been through. Besides, I am starting to feel goose pimples across my skin. I press on again through the water, doing breast-stroke this time, and allow myself one more passage back and forth before I swim towards the shore and make my way through the water to the sand, and back to our little spot. Ben and Holly are sweetly wrapped in their beach blankets, sucking juice from cartons, while Sam is cracking open a beer for Ron.

"Mummy!" Ben shouts. "Ron and me made a whole citadel!"

"Wow, that sounds amazing, you'll have to show me," I say, wrapping a towel around myself.

Karen sits up and smiles at me. "I bet that did you some good."

"It was amazing, thank you," I say. "Just what the doctor ordered."

Sam offers me a beer as well. It's just a small one and, while I don't normally drink beer, the sight of the cold green bottle is enticing. "Yes, please."

He hands it to me and raises his so that I can clink mine against it. "Cheers. Here's to summer."

"To summer," I smile, and lift the bottle to my lips.

Karen pulls a box of sandwiches and a multi-pack of crisps from her oversized bag, and we sit on our blankets, not bothered that there is sand everywhere.

"There is just nothing quite like a picnic on the beach," I say.

"I know. This is pretty much perfect," says Sam.

We stay for another hour or so; it is well past the children's bedtime, but it's too lovely an evening to miss. Mum and

Dad come to join us as well, and as the beach all but empties, we play football and frisbee, until Holly is in tears, and I scoop her up and let her fall asleep on my lap while the others run around with Ben, who is laughing and delighted to have the attention of nearly all the adults.

Eventually, we have to give in, and reluctantly pack up our things. Karen and Ron say their goodbyes and head off to the Mainbrace for a 'swift half' (yeah, right), and Mum stays with us while Dad goes to get his car. We squeeze in, Mum closing the door behind us and blowing us kisses before she walks back to the hotel and Dad takes us home.

I unlock the door, to be greeted by an excited Meg, and Sam carries in a still-sleeping Holly while Ben wraps his arms and legs around Dad. He is still just about awake enough to giggle as Dad jiggles him up and down, making clip-clop noises. I want to say not to wake him up too much, but I am also feeling relaxed and happy and like I really don't care. It's been so nice to all be together, enjoying ourselves. I just smile, and kiss Ben as Dad trots him past me.

"Want me to read to you, Benny?" Dad asks.

"Yes!"

"Night, night, Ben," I say, kissing my little boy on his nose.

"Night, Mummy."

"Looks like it's just you and me then, Meg," I say. With Sam sorting out Holly – trying to change her nappy and get her into pyjamas while she stays asleep is no mean feat – and Dad reading to Ben, I go into the lounge and open the French doors. Meg goes outside while I flop onto the settee. No TV, no book, no nothing. Just me, the very vague breeze which filters in through the open doors, and the sounds of the summer.

5

"David!" I exclaim, seeing his US number on my screen. It's always a treat to hear from my old friend, and I miss him very much. He and Martin and the kids were meant to have returned to Cornwall last year, but with 'the covid situation', they had decided to stay put. David's sister, my old boss Bea, was delighted, of course. She is in the States long-term, married to American Bob, so having her brother out there for longer than planned has been a real blessing to her. But his return is imminent; just in time for the festival, in fact, and I cannot wait. "I was just thinking about you," I say now, although in truth I hadn't been. I had been lying on my back, on the settee, trying to keep my eyelids from fluttering and lulling me into a premature sleep. "Counting the days till I see you!"

"Alice," his voice cuts right through my cheer.

"What?" I say, sitting up sharply, images of Martin and the kids in a car crash, or David getting a cancer diagnosis. The tone of his voice, with just that one word, leaves me in no doubt that something serious has happened.

"It's Bob," he says, and to my shame I experience a very slight relief. I do love Bob, but mostly because he loves Bea, and makes her so happy, but I don't know him brilliantly well. And at least it's not David, I think. I can't help it. After Julie, he is my best friend. If you don't count Sam. And I don't really; Sam is on another level. Nevertheless, a little chill runs over me, hot on the heels of the initial relief.

"What is it? What's wrong?"

"He's got covid," David says, "and I don't just mean the flu-kind. Or the 'I hardly noticed I had it' kind. He's got it bad. He's in hospital, in intensive care."

"Oh," I breathe. "Oh no. That's terrible." And my feelings catch up with me. My real, genuine feelings, and I'm pleased that they've come back in line. "How is he? If that's not a stupid question."

"He's pretty bad, I think. And we can't see him. Not even Bea. Nobody's allowed on the covid wards. She's got it herself as well, so I can't even go and see her, and be with her. I have to stay away."

"Oh my god." The severity of the situation settles over me and I find myself and my mood falling from the positivity of earlier to the stark reality of my friends' circumstances.

"I mean, she couldn't go in and see him anyway," David continues, his voice small, "but I could at least have gone to be with her. Or she could have come to stay with us…"

"I know. I know." I try to soothe him. A thought strikes me. "Is Bea very ill?"

"She's not great," he says, "but not awful. At least, not at the moment. Says she feels flucy, and she's got a bad cough. But Bob started out like that, too. What if something happens to Bea, Alice?" Bea and David's parents died a long time ago and Bea, a good few years older than her brother, has always been quite maternal towards him. He relies on her heavily, although she also relies on him, far more than she might admit.

"I don't know," I say, not wishing to glibly say that

nothing will happen to her. That she isn't going to get any worse. I clutch at a pathetic straw: "Bob's older than her, though, isn't he?"

"Yes. And he's had some problems with his heart," David acknowledges.

"Has he?"

"Yes, well, some time ago. He was a chain-smoker, apparently – hence his gorgeous gruff voice! – and a bit of a hard drinker too; all according to him. He settled down, though, and he's really tried to look after himself these last few years. And he looks after Bea, and makes her so happy."

I can hear in David's voice that he is close to tears. I stay quiet for a few moments, to allow him space to speak again if he wants to, but all I can hear now is a slight snuffling sound. I wish so much that I could be there with him.

"David," I say, sounding more confident than I am. "It might all be OK. I know it must be really hard not being able to see him, and really scary, too. But they know so much more about covid now than they did at first. They know how it affects people, and how to treat it. And the hospitals aren't as rushed off their feet as they were, at least not in the UK. I assume that's the same in the States?"

"Yes, it's true. Very true," he replies, almost politely.

"So, hopefully they'll sort him out. People do recover from covid, you know. Even people who have been in comas for weeks. Not that I think that will happen to Bob. He's not, is he? In a coma, I mean?"

"No, he's not. He's conscious. And Bea's spoken to him on FaceTime, she says he looks awful."

"I'm not surprised. He must have it bad if he's in intensive care. But hopefully they'll have him out of there soon."

"Hopefully," David agrees. I feel like he's not buying my positivity. Which is not like him at all. "But Alice, I am going to have to stay on, you know. I can't leave Bea now."

"Oh. Oh yes, of course." I fill with selfish disappointment, but I shrug it off quickly. This is not about me.

"Martin and the kids will be coming back, though."

"Really?"

"Yes. He's got to get back for work. We've delayed enough already, and they need him in the UK now. I want the kids to stay here, but we've already given in our notice on the house, and I'm going to stay with Bea as long as she needs me, once she's clear of covid, of course. There's not space there for the kids, and I think they need to come home, too. They need to get back to their friends over there, and settle before the school year starts."

"Who's going to look after them, if Martin's working?"

"Jill and Graham said they'll do it. They can't wait, in fact!" His voice brightens a little. Martin's parents are lovely people, and have missed their son and their grandchildren, and their son-in-law, a lot. "But I did wonder if you'd have them to your place every now and then, to see your two, and help them ease back into normal life again?"

"Of course!" I say, with no hesitation. It's been a long while since I last saw Tyler and Esme, and as I remember it, Tyler was a bit of a handful, but he's older now and according to Martin and David, he's settled down a lot. Anyway, I would do anything to help them out.

"Thanks, Alice. And hopefully Bob will be on the mend soon, and I'll be flying back to join you all."

"Yes!" I say. "Exactly. I guess you're going to miss the festival, though."

"Well, I expect they'll delay it for my return. It is all about me, isn't it?"

"Yes, yes, of course it is!" I laugh. And I think of something to cheer him up, telling him about Crazy Craig's Castles. Not in a mean way; Craig seems like a lovely man, but I know that it will tickle David, and I do an exaggerated impression of Craig's Brummie accent, knowing it will make him laugh.

"He sounds amazing!" David says. "I know what we're doing for the kids' birthdays! Oh, looks like Bea's trying to get through. I'd better go, Alice. Love you."

"Love you, too. Thank you for letting me know about Bob. And give Bea my love…" But David's already hung up.

"That's awful," Sam says, when I tell him and Dad.

"Nasty business, this," Dad says. "I'm still scared of it, I can tell you. I don't care what people say. This virus hasn't gone away."

I know it bothers him, having people coming into and out of the Sail Loft, travelling from all different parts of the country, and then traversing around the town. It's been impossible not to do it, though, as business has been tough enough, and the support from the government is gradually ebbing away. We have very strict cleaning controls at Amethi, and we have had to increase our prices to cover these extra costs – as have many self-catering places and especially hotels and B&Bs. We need to make sure that our guests are safe, and our staff, and ourselves. At least at Amethi everyone is more or less self-contained, and in between guests we can thoroughly air the properties. For Mum and Dad at the Sail Loft, they have to share spaces with their guests, and of course cook and serve breakfasts. The windows are open most of the time, but that brings its own problems, when there's a particularly stiff breeze blowing in from the sea.

"I know," I say to Dad. "I'm amazed Bob's the first person we know to have really been affected by it."

"I hope he's OK," says Sam.

"Yeah," I say glumly. "Me too."

It would be easy to think all will come right, and tell ourselves to think positive, but sometimes it's not as simple as that.

6

There is quite a buzz around town in the week approaching the festival. It reminds me of how it felt at school when the end of the year was approaching. A kind of heady, giggly, high-spiritedness. It's all anyone is talking about, and it's such a lovely contrast to last year, when the main topics were, of course, covid, and the expected onslaught of tourists.

I don't know who came up with the idea of this festival; it came out of one of the town council meetings, I believe, and it soon took hold. Almost everybody wants to be involved. The primary school is opening its doors, with the hall being requisitioned for a whole day's programme of music, from the school band and choir to the more grown-up community choir and silver band, and later in the evening some of the local bands and musicians will be playing. The little buses which nip up and down between the top and bottom of town will be running for free, with reduced passenger numbers – and the ubiquitous face masks of course – so that people can take the weight of their feet, and enjoy being ferried about between the different events that are taking place.

The raffle is by now absolutely enormous, and it has been decided that the draw will take place the following day, or it might take forever to read out all the winners' names.

The rugby club has been primed for the fairground. The recent long spell of warm weather has dried out the pitch, to the relief of the rugby club committee, and Gary, the coach, who has been assured that there is funding available to help bring it back to order in time for rugby practice resuming.

Up at Amethi, we are putting the finishing touches to the solstice yoga retreat. We have done it a number of times now, and have learned what does and doesn't work. It is a fairly simple formula, really: lovely food, a well-planned programme, and plenty of opportunities for guests to socialise, or just chill out on their own. The main problem is that the day that the solstice falls on keeps moving. Very inconvenient! We have to plan around this. This year, it is a Monday, so where other retreats have focused on the solstice as a fitting ending, this year it will be at the start of the course, as the guests only arrive on the Sunday. Last year would have been extra difficult, but we decided against holding it last year (all together now… *because of covid*).

Lizzie is, of course, unfazed by it. "It will fall when it falls," she says, and I think, *Well yes, of course it will*. But I know what she means. I think she enjoys the challenge, of being able to tailor the course to each changing year.

"I think we'll have an early evening session on Sunday night, to get everyone nice and chilled, and be up early for the Monday morning, taking it easy through the day. Focusing on the healing positivity of the sun. We can end with the bonfire, and maybe go for a lighter meal this time, Julie. Then a later start on Tuesday, and more normal hours on Wednesday, before the last night meal and an early session Thursday morning before they all go. Maybe we can still have a celebration feast on the last night, instead of on the solstice itself. I don't want people overdoing it early on!"

"That sounds perfect, Lizzie, I can do that," says Julie. "We'll make it a whole week of celebrations. It's just what people need."

"Definitely," Lizzie enthuses. "The focus is going to be on positivity and hope, letting them feel the warmth and nourishment from the sun."

"Sounds lovely," I say. "I wish I was on this retreat."

"Well, make sure you get to at least some of the sessions, you two."

"We will."

"And the bonfire?"

"Of course! Sam's got the whole week off, with it being Ben's birthday as well, so I'm free to come up for the whole thing on the Monday, as long as I wake up when my alarm goes off."

"You will," Lizzie smiles.

"I'll do my best."

All our properties are full this week, and booked well into the autumn. It's a bumper year, and just what we need, to try and get us back on the straight and narrow. We managed last year, but only broke even, really. Mum and Dad had a harder time, but they're in the privileged position of having some money to fall back on. The Sail Loft is hard work, and maybe for them the lockdowns were a blessing as well, in a way. A chance to regroup and recuperate. Of course, they couldn't sit still, and decided to refresh their décor. Nothing major, as my friend Sarah had already done the interior design just a few years back, but they redid the paint jobs, and did some major work on the garden, which looks fantastic. Lucky us, that our businesses have come through the hardest year almost unscathed. Others have not been so lucky. And others still have taken the opportunity to hike their prices so as to be unaffordable for many. A bitter pill for locals and regular visitors alike. But for others, unsure of whether or not they might go on their usual all-inclusive holiday abroad; if it might be cancelled or cut short because of changes to which countries we are and are not allowed to visit, Cornwall has become one of the destinations of choice.

It's also been extremely well publicised because of the G7 summit which has just taken place – images of the most powerful people in the world posing and gallivanting on our gleaming beaches and sparkling seas have been broadcast internationally – and it has fixed this beautiful place even more firmly onto the map. There are many, many people who will pay crazy prices and accept that is just the way it is. The term 'staycation', which meant taking a few days off but staying at home and having day trips, has been hijacked, and now is being used to describe what has always previously been known as a 'holiday'.

There are so many things, good and bad, to have come from this strange time we are living through. Neighbours have become more important, as people have begun to socialise on their streets – bringing out deckchairs and sun loungers to their driveways, pavements, front yards, and enjoying a cuppa, or a beer, with people they may have previously been too busy to stop and chat with. Shopping is being done for those too old, frail, at risk, or even afraid, to go to enclosed public spaces. Cafes are delivering meals, restaurants sending in takeaways for NHS staff. There is kindness and generosity amidst the fear, and long may it last.

Julie and I will be up at Amethi on Saturday morning, seeing off our current guests, then working with Cindy to deep-clean the cottages. We will head back home about mid-day and have lunch, then meet again, with Luke and Sam and the kids – including Sophie, who's coming down from Devon by train in the morning – and head into town. Sam is taking Meg to Mum and Dad's so that she has some company, and so that we don't have to rush back for her. My parents are resolutely staying put, not wanting to risk the crowds.

"We can hear it all from the garden," Dad said when we dropped by last weekend. "I'm not worried about missing out. I mean, it'll be nice to hear it going on, but you know I'm getting on a bit. And I don't get enough time relaxing out here these days. Seems like somebody's always nicking my seat."

He looked across to the decking that he had built during the first lockdown. Ben and Holly had requisitioned the loungers, and were reclining, wearing their grandparents' oversized sunglasses. It had been Ben's idea, and Holly, as ever, was game for anything he suggested.

"Plus, he's spent all his money on raffle tickets!" Mum laughed. "Fifty quid!"

"Have you, Dad?"

"Yeah, I want to win that meal from Julie and you!"

"Oh god, I hadn't thought of that. Hopefully you'll get a set of gel nails from Tiana instead."

"I could do with brightening myself up," he examined his hands thoughtfully.

"Fingers crossed, then."

"That would make doing my nails a bit difficult."

"Dad jokes," I had sighed. "Sam's still got a way to go before he reaches your standard, but he's getting there."

"Hey! I heard that," said Sam.

"You were meant to."

"Anyway, they're giving rain for Saturday," Dad continued, "so we might be watching from inside."

"I did hear that," I looked out across the familiar view of the town, soaked in sunshine. "Hard to imagine, isn't it? It feels like it will never rain again!"

"Hopefully it won't reach us down here. It's meant to be much worse up country," Mum said. "Listen to me, I sound like a proper local!"

"Not with your accent, Sue," Sam said.

"Watch it, you! I was going to say you can come and shelter here if it does get bad, but I can always change my mind…"

I'll be glad to know that Meg is being looked after on Saturday. She can lounge around in the garden with Mum and Dad, and no doubt allow herself to be fussed over the fence by any passing dog-lovers. It means that we are free to go out for as long as we please, and as long as the kids will tolerate. There will be fireworks once it's dark, and Meg hates those, so I couldn't have allowed her to be on her own, but now she can stay inside with Mum, who is also not a fan, while Dad can lie on his lounger and *ooh* and *ahh* to his heart's content.

The undercurrent of enthusiasm is definitely catching, and I can't wait for Saturday!

7

"Have you seen the sky?" Julie says at lunchtime on Friday, peering out of the office window. There is a definite chill in the air, compared to how it's been in recent weeks, and the breeze ripples in through the window, agitating the pile of papers on my desk.

I look out. Above our colourful wildflower meadows, and beyond the line of protective trees that form the boundary to Amethi, all is grey and brooding. "Urgh," I say to the clouds, "get lost! We could do without this, although maybe we can get it out of the way today, so that tomorrow's clear for the festival."

"Was that a rumble?" Julie asks.

"Not thunder?"

"It wasn't forecast. Probably just a big lorry up the road or something."

"I hope so."

I think a couple of summers back, to when Sam had his accident, on a rain-sodden, stormy night. Now, when I see skies like these, it brings it all back to me. It had been Jonathan who was our primary concern that night, and only when he'd turned up at our door had we realised that it was in fact Sam who was missing. Sam who had fallen down the cliff – although we didn't know that at first, of course.

The terrifying car journey up to the hospital, knowing

Sam had been airlifted there. The relief at discovering that, although badly injured, he was alive, he was OK, and he would recover. It took him a while, but he got there, and in the background I had to manage my own anxiety and shock, which doubled when I discovered I was pregnant for the second time. Luckily, with Ben and Holly to keep me busy, I don't have a lot of time for reflection and thinking what might have been. I have no choice but to move forward. But even so, these kinds of stormy, moody skies represent more than a grey, damp day – a ruined festival – to me.

"Ah! The food delivery," Julie says, as we hear the familiar crunch of gravel as the van arrives in the car park.

"Excellent! I'll come and help you check through everything. Age before beauty," I say, gesturing for her to go before me.

"Ladies first, you mean," says Julie.

"If it makes you feel better, sure."

I follow her down, and she stops in the doorway. "Oh no."

"What?"

"Rain."

"Noooooo."

Fat drops of water plop onto the gravel, which has been dry for weeks; each making its mark like a tear.

"I knew it," Julie says.

"Let's just hope it passes. Look, there's a patch of blue over there."

"I'm not seeing it, Griffiths… I mean, Branvall…" she says. "You always say there's blue sky."

"That's because I am an eternal optimist, and you are a grumpy pessimist."

"Realist, more like."

"Whatever. Come on, let's get this food in, before it really starts."

Despite the fact that I really, really do not want it to rain, the smell that it evokes is welcome – like a re-awakening of the plants, and the earth. I breathe in deeply as I follow hot on Julie's heels. We round the corner to find Carrie the delivery driver already shifting two heavy crates around the side of the building.

"Bloody hell… Carrie by name, carry by nature," Julie says – as she does every week.

"Just let her past, Julie," I say. "Are you alright, Carrie? We'll go and grab some things, too."

"Great, you are both stars! All of your stuff's stacked just inside the truck. All marked Amethi too, mind, so don't go nicking anyone else's."

"Not even the Sail Loft's?"

"Especially not! Your mum'd have my guts for garters!"

Julie and I can only manage one crate each, and we have just got them into the kitchen when Carrie arrives with her next pair.

"How do you do it, Carrie?"

"Cornish, see. Strong. Not like you two."

"I wish I hadn't asked."

She hands Julie the manifest. "Get checking through this, and I'll bring the last two crates, OK?"

"Yes, boss."

When Carrie comes back this time, her short blonde hair is soaking.

"Just got me!" she breathes. "You don't want to go out there right now." She is breathing heavily.

"Oh bugger," I say. "Please tell me it's just passing over."

47

"Hope so."

While Julie unpacks the boxes, ticking items off her list, I pour Carrie a glass of water. "Will you be going to the festival tomorrow?"

"Course! Wouldn't miss it." She gulps her drink down. "Best be off now, though, if you've got everything."

Julie looks up. "Looks good to me, Carrie."

She stacks all the empty crates together, and is gone.

For the rest of the afternoon, the rain keeps on coming, and is joined by a stern wind sent from the sea. I go outside to cover up the outdoor furniture, and make sure there's nothing likely to blow around and cause any damage. There are a couple of gusts that take my breath away.

"This is ridiculous!" I say to Julie, rubbing my hair with a towel as I come into the kitchen to let her know all is as planned for dinner. "They didn't say it would be this bad." Outside, the gravel is literally swimming in water now, all traces of dust washed away. Our poor guests - this being the last day of their holiday, and they are confined indoors.

"I know," she says, chopping the heads off a bunch of carrots. "But maybe it's a blessing, it will all be over in time for tomorrow."

"Not such a pessimist, after all!" I grin. "Motherhood's really softened you up, my friend. It is grim right now, though. The rugby ground's going to take a pounding. I saw all the trucks and the rides arriving last night. They'll have been setting up today, and I think they were planning to open tonight."

"Imagine the carnage! Thank god the kids are too young to want to go!"

"And we're too old…"

"Sad but true! Now go on, get away with you, your kids will be waiting! I'll see you here bright and early."

"Early, at least."

My windscreen wipers are going ten to the dozen as I leave the Amethi driveway. Away from the shelter of our protective line of trees, I realise we really have got a bit of a storm going on. It's part and parcel of living by the sea, and I'm often struck by the way that weather is so key to life and events here; it affects livelihoods, in terms of the fishing fleet, and the farmers, and it affects tourism trade and shop footfall. On a pleasant sunny afternoon, Fore Street will be swarming with people, ambling along hand-in-hand, stopping to gaze into shop windows and deciding they will treat themselves to that necklace/jumper/art print that they really can't afford, as a memento of their time here. Days like this, however, see people sitting indoors, making the most of time to read, or watch the holiday accommodation TV streaming services. Pubs, cafes and restaurants still do well, but the streets are comparatively empty, with people dashing through from necessity, hoods up, coats pulled tightly around them, spare hands trying to stop umbrellas turning inside-out, which really is a thankless task on a day like today.

My drive back to town is pretty open to the elements, and there's a point where I can see the sea, and, as I expected, it is grey to match the sky, and very unsettled. I know it's high tide fairly late tonight, so with a bit of luck everything will be a bit more settled by then.

I arrive at Goslings to find that apparently everybody has

driven to pick their children up. Fair enough – I've done the same – but there is a queue of cars waiting to get into the small car park. I fiddle with my radio while I wait, and find the local station.

"Thank you, Craig, it's been lovely to have you on our show this afternoon. I appreciate your honesty, and I'm sure many of our listeners will, too."

"Thank you for having me, Grace."

I recognise that voice. I am sure I do. It's got to be Crazy Craig. I wonder what he's been talking about. Maybe what it's like to move here. Or the trials and tribulations of a bouncy castle business owner. The car in front moves forward, and I edge along as well.

The DJ plays Kate Bush *This Woman's Work*, which never fails to bring tears to my eyes. I'm grateful for the rain falling, and obscuring the view of me wiping them away.

It's just another few minutes before I pull into a parking space and dash across to the front door, to collect Ben and Holly, who are standing obediently, Ben grasping a flag he has coloured in and stuck to a plastic stick – "For the festival, Mummy, look!" – while Holly immediately puts her arms up to me to be picked up.

"Thanks so much, Amy," I say to the woman dishing out children to parents and carers. "See you at the festival?"

"Yes! As long as this lot's cleared by then," she gestures to the moody sky.

"It will," I say. "It has to!"

"I hope you're right."

Back home, Meg barks a welcome to us as we bustle into the hallway. I put Ben's flag in a vase on the windowsill, and deposit Holly on the kitchen floor so that I can open the door for Meg. She stands keenly by, eager to go out, then at first sight of the weather she retreats a little, her pressing need no longer quite so urgent. The garden is well protected by high fences, against which we have grown clematis, and tomato plants. I pull my hood up and step outside to entice Meg out and, as I do, it feels like the heavens really open, and a deluge of rain begins. Meg is watching me from just inside the doorway. "Fine," I say to her. "You'll just have to cross your legs." I come back in, glad to shut the door behind me, and happy we have nowhere else to be for the rest of the day. I'm guessing the fair won't be open tonight after all, and I hope they can keep the ground in relatively good condition for tomorrow. It's been so very dry lately that, although it is properly tipping it down now, if it runs its course soon, the ground might well soak all of this much-needed moisture up, like a giant sponge, and all being well we will awake to bright blue skies tomorrow.

I had hoped to get the kids and Meg down to the beach this afternoon, but instead we end up playing various boxed games, nice and simple for Holly, but even so Ben ends up getting cross when she knocks down the hanging monkeys on purpose, one too many times.

"Alright," I give in. "Let's put on the TV. And I'll get us an early tea."

I like the idea of them having an early night and a good sleep before tomorrow, but experience tells me this is never a guarantee. Still, I manage to get tea and baths done before half past six, when Sam should be home. He's gone by bike today, and I imagine he's wishing that he hadn't. By quarter to seven, he's still not back, and I look out of the window for him. It's still tipping it down, and the trees on the other side of the street are being knocked about by the wind.

"Rain, rain, go away," I say.

Ben finishes it off: "Come back another day!"

I smile and hug him, lifting him to the window just in time to see Sam arrive, his soaking cycling gear clinging to him. We wave, and the kids run to the doorway.

"Stand back," I say, as Sam comes in, and even Meg backs away from this sodden cyclist.

"Is it raining out?" I ask.

"You've noticed, have you?" Sam smiles, kisses me and the kids, lightly, so as not to soak us. "I'm going to have to take this lot off right here," he says, "or I'll drip all over the house." He begins to pull his clothes off, shaking his hair at the kids and making them run shrieking and laughing into the lounge.

"I'll grab you a towel," I say, and run upstairs to the bathroom, where I decide maybe a few towels would be better. A brief memory passes through my mind. Sam arriving drenched at David's house, back when Julie and I rented the very top rooms there. It was the day that May, Luke's mum, had died, and Sam had taken Julie to see Luke, then he'd come back to see me. A hot bath, overflowing with bubbles. He'd invited me to join him…

But this is not a memory for now. Now, we are old and married, and responsible parents, and dog owners. I turn on the shower for him, and rush back down with the towels. "Go on up and warm up," I say. "A hot shower should sort you out."

"It's a nightmare out there," he says. "Run-off water everywhere, I'm glad I didn't have to go through town."

I used to quite like a rainy day when I lived in David's old house – the steep street would host two narrow, bubbling streams, running down either side of it, from the top of town towards the harbour. I could sit at the little window in my room and look down, safe and snug, and glad I wasn't one of the people scurrying along below.

"I bet it's wild down there."

"It will be, have you seen the sea?"

"I had a little glimpse of it earlier. Is it bad?"

"Pretty rough at the minute."

"I'm glad you're back," I hug him, not minding that my clothes are now wet, too. "I'm going to put my pyjamas on, and get the kids to bed, and then we can have tea."

"Sounds perfect. What Friday nights were made for."

"Oh, we are very dull, aren't we?"

"I prefer to think of it as happy," says Sam.

Both bedtimes go well. Ben sits in his bed, looking at a book while I read to Holly, and, as ever, it doesn't take long for her to fall asleep. I kiss her and turn her light down low, then go through to see Ben. I spend longer with him, as he likes to chat at bedtime, and normally has a whole array of questions for me.

"Is it still raining, Mummy?"

I stand and open his curtains a little. It's light, but dark, the glowering clouds overbearing. It is indeed still raining.

"It is, Benny. But hopefully it will stop soon."

"Can I have my flag?"

"Can I have my flag what?" I prompt.

"Can I have my flag upstairs?" He looks at me. Senses there is still something missing. "Sorry?"

I laugh, and he tries again. "Thank you?"

"That's good enough!" I smile. "Go on, then." I go onto the landing, catching a glimpse of Sam in our room, pulling a jumper over his head. I allow myself a moment to admire his back, before running my errand. I pretend-pant as I get back to Ben's room. "Here… you are… Ben…"

"You're silly, Mummy," he laughs, and he puts his arm out; a sign for me to lie down next to him, his little arm around my shoulders, like he's the parent and I'm the child. He strokes my hair. I close my eyes briefly, and try to make a mental imprint of this very moment. Life is so hectic and full, I have to remind myself to stop sometimes and appreciate times like this. Be in the moment, as Lizzie says.

"Now read," Ben withdraws his embrace, and adds, "please."

"OK!" I laugh and sit up, finding his book on the shelf above the bed. He has no idea just how important these times are to me, but I hope one day when he's older he will occasionally look back and remember them.

I read to Ben about a family of pirates who move into a seaside town and befriend a young girl living there. "Are there pirates here, Mummy?"

"Not anymore," I say. "Not like these ones, anyway! But I bet there'll people dressed up like pirates at the festival tomorrow."

"Can I dress up?"

"If you like. As a pirate?" My mind scans our dressing-up box. I'm not sure we've got anything suitable.

"No, Spiderman."

I laugh again. "Of course." That will be much easier.

"Right. Time to sleep, Ben."

"Has it stopped raining yet?"

"I don't suppose it will have. But I'll check." A cursory glance outside tells me it is still raining, although perhaps a little less hard than it was earlier. "I think it's going to stop soon, Ben."

"I hope so."

"Me, too." I kiss him, and his toy tiger, and leave the room. I have curry in mind, and maybe an early night for Sam and me, too.

8

By the time we go to bed, the rain finally seems to be showing signs of abating.

"Thank god for that," I say to Sam, hooking the curtain back with my finger. "I just hope it dries up a bit for tomorrow."

"It will," he says, already in bed. He's started having to wear glasses for reading and he's got them on now. I like them.

"You look quite sexy in your glasses," I say.

"Only in my glasses?"

"Yep. Otherwise – just plain ugly."

"Right. You'd better come here and say that."

I climb on the bed next to him. "Just plain ugly," I say again, and I laugh as he grabs me playfully, pushing me down on top of the covers, and rolling on top of me. He takes off his glasses.

"Urgh, don't! I can't look. It's even worse close up!"

His blue eyes laugh down at me, and he reaches across to put the glasses on his bedside table, then he's back, and he's kissing me, and I'm remembering how nice it is to be kissed. It's funny, when you think about what it's like when you first get together with somebody. You kiss all the time. You can't stop, like it's a physical need. And all the other stuff, whenever you get to that point. It's addictive. That one person occupies a huge proportion of your time, both physically and mentally – emotionally, too. I know every relationship is different, but I suspect that for most of us it is safe to say that, over time, this changes. The physical need is not as urgent, and other aspects of life creep in: work; money; family; friends; children. And as their little tendrils curl around your mind, hooking into your consciousness, they start to pull you back, and that feeling of cleverness at having found each other diminishes. The love changes, but it doesn't have to be any less. Just different.

It's just times like now that remind me how good it still feels, to be physically close, and to lose ourselves in each other. Sam's kiss slides across to my earlobe, and I can hear his breath; feel its softness on my skin. I smile, and I put my hand in his hair, feeling the familiar curls.

Bbbrrrrrrrr…. Bbbrrrrrrrr…. His phone starts vibrating, on his bedside table, and I hear his glasses fall to the floor.

"Bugger," he breathes, still right next to my ear.

"Ignore it," I say.

The call rings out, and we smile at each other. Sam's mouth finds mine again.

Bbbrrrrrrrr…. Bbbrrrrrrrr….

"FFS." Sam and I started using this handy text-talk abbreviation in front of the kids, and now as a matter of course. "I'd better see who it is." He leans over, the majority of his body still across mine. He groans. "I should have known. It's Mum."

"At this time of night?"

Karen has an annoying habit of ringing and then, if the call is not answered, trying again straight after. Sam turns the phone to silent, but now I'm thinking. Although she is a persistent caller, Karen is unlikely to ring at this time of night without good reason. And as Sam begins kissing me all over again, I find I can't shake the thought that there might be something wrong.

"I think you should call her back," I say.

"What? No," Sam says, kissing my jawline. "She'll leave a message if it's important."

Both he and I know this is not true. She will just keep on ringing. And I imagine her frustration if she is doing that now and not getting through.

That's the other thing about losing that urgency of a new relationship: it is very easy to go off the boil. I kiss Sam, then gently push myself away a little. "Just call her. Make sure she's OK. Then we can get back to this."

"Do I have to?"

"Yes. I think so."

"Alright." Sam shifts himself across the bed, sitting up and putting his glasses back on. He looks over the top of them at me and grins.

"You look sexy again now," I say.

He picks up his phone. "Will wonders never cease? She's actually left a message." He dials voicemail, and listens. I watch his face. His expression changes to one of concern.

"What is it?" I ask, immediately nervous. It's a horrible way to think, but we're at this age now; our parents, too, when I feel like life is a little more precarious. Mum had the scare with her heart a few years ago, and of course Luke's mum died even before that, although she was really unfairly young. Maybe it's the pandemic that's brought on this feeling of impending doom, but it's never all that far away. "Is she OK?"

Sam nods, looking serious, and listening. "Shit."

"What?" I say. Could it be Ron? I really hope not.

"Town's flooded. Low town, at least. And there's been some incident. The lifeboat's out. Some guy taking photos, too close to the edge of the harbour. He was knocked off his feet, and swept into the sea."

Urgh. I feel a physical and mental jolt at the thought of it. "Oh my god. That's awful." That doesn't even cover it.

We both know it's stupid, being reckless near the sea. Lots of people do it, when the waves are wild. Trying to get a good shot – or even trying just to feel that wildness of the water. I do think there is something in that – the absolute lack of control we have over these things, when so much else in life is about order and organisation. But right now, it doesn't matter whether the man was being careless or thoughtless; he is in the cold, cold water, and god knows what will be happening to him, or what state he will be in. I just hope that the lifeboat will get to him; although of course in doing so, they'll be putting themselves in danger.

There was a time when Sam had plans to become a lifeboat crew member, but his accident put paid to that idea and, selfishly, I was relieved. Ron has done his time, too, and his age and encroaching arthritis mean he is now confined to shore as well.

"I'd better get down there," says Sam.

"But what can you do? I mean, I really hope they find him, but you can't really do anything."

"No, I know. But it sounds like they might need help sorting things out with the flooding as well."

"Of course." I had not really registered that part. "Is it very bad?"

"According to Mum, yes. The high tide and the rainfall, and the waves have done it. It'll be the drains, too. We've been saying for ages they need to sort them out. Something was bound to happen."

"But it's the festival tomorrow," I say, immediately berating myself for being so pathetic. A man's life is in the balance, and people's properties are flooding. What does the festival matter? Only it does matter, because it's not really about the raffle, or the fairground, or the music, food and drink. It's about giving us all something to feel happy about again, and rediscovering that sense of joy. From what Sam's said, I don't think that is going to happen now, and my heart sinks.

It's crazy how things can turn round in a moment.

As Sam starts to get dressed, I pull a hoodie on over my pyjamas, and I follow him downstairs.

"I wish I could come too," I say. I would like to see for myself what is going on, and work out how to help. Maybe, just maybe, it won't be as bad as all that. But in my heart, I know that it will.

9

I don't know what to do with myself. I can't possibly go to sleep. And I can't call Sam, as no doubt he will be in the midst of things. They'll hopefully have known something was coming, and have had the sandbags out, at the very least. But if town's been hit from both sides, with the rain coming down and the drains bursting, plus the sea giving it all it's got, then I fear for some of the buildings and businesses along the sea front.

But most pressing is this man who's been washed out to sea. The thought of it; how utterly terrifying it must be. And how confusing, getting tumbled around underwater, not knowing which way is up. Or bashed against the rocks. I feel serious shivers at the thought of it. And I worry for the lifeboat crew, as well. How ridiculously brave they are.

I make a cup of tea, and I curl up on the settee. Meg jumps up gently to join me, and her weight and warmth are a comfort. I put on my laptop to find the local news website, because even though this is a huge thing here, it is unlikely to be hitting the national news just yet.

There are live reports of flooding all along the coast, and our lifeboat is not the only one that's been scrambled. Images start to come in, and I watch keenly for those of the town I love. Soon enough, there is some video footage. I watch, mesmerised, as I see what is happening literally five minutes down the road from here. Flashing blue lights rebounding off walls and shop windows. Waters sloshing up and over the sides of the harbour, encroaching on the cobbled road, pulling a large black bin back with them. The waves get bigger, and throw themselves into the air; a display of bravado to the onlookers who, despite the risks, stand by, watching and exclaiming at each new, bigger explosion of water and foam.

The water has found its way along the narrow passageway behind the public toilets, and it pours down the roads from higher up. Meeting on the flat surfaces of the lower town, rushing along the streets. People stand inside their shops and cafes, barricaded by sandbags but keeping watch as the waters do their best to break in.

I message Julie:

Have you seen?

Yes. Nightmare.

Has Luke gone down?

Yep. Sam?

Yes. Of course. Urgh, it's horrible.

I know. I hope that guy's OK.

Me too. I'm going to check in with Mum and Dad now.

Alright… give me a bell in a bit if you like. I don't think I'll be getting much sleep. xx

Will do xx

I text Mum. I wonder if she and Dad might already be asleep and missing what's going on. But of course they're not.

Everything OK at the Sail Loft, Mum?

At the top of town, I know it won't be in any danger from flooding.

Yes, thanks, Alice. But isn't it awful? We're keeping the doors open in case anyone needs some shelter, or even just a cup of tea.

This makes me smile. **I am sure that will be appreciated xx**

It's the least we can do. It sounds like they've got that man, though. And he's alive, thank god.

Thank god, I agree, and try not to wonder how it is that Mum has got this news before me. Obviously, my parents' placing on the town grapevine is not the important thing right now.

But those poor people down there. There's no telling what's happening to their businesses.

Fingers crossed it will pass with minimal damage.

Let's hope so.

Love you, Mum xx

Love you, too xx

I let the news sink in that they have already managed to rescue the man from the sea. I hope he's OK, and I hope the lifeboat doesn't have to be called out again. I decide to stop checking for news. Sam will be in touch soon, and let me know how things are. Instead, I put on the TV, and stick *Friends* on Netflix. I've watched all the episodes so many times over the years, but I feel like right now calls for comfort TV of the highest order. However, at the sound of the American accents, my mind flicks to Bob, and Bea. What time will it be there now? Around lunchtime, I guess. I wonder what Bea is doing. I decide to give her a ring, on the off-chance she is free and needs a chat.

"Hello?" her familiar voice sends my mind skidding back across the years. She was my first boss here, when she owned the Sail Loft, which she had built up single-handedly after her first marriage broke down. I was quite scared of her, then. She seemed so confident, and sure of herself. I could never have imagined being like that, and I was nervous around her, which probably made me more accident-prone than I would have been otherwise. She was always kind, though, even in the case of the occasional breakage. As long as her guests were happy, she was, she would say. Now, she sounds doubtful. Fearful. I realise she must be constantly expecting a call from the hospital.

"Bea, it's Alice," I say as quickly as I can.

"Oh, Alice! How lovely to hear from you," she says immediately, but she must be both relieved and disappointed it's not somebody more important.

"I'm sorry to phone with no warning," I say. "And I don't want to tie up your phoneline…"

"Oh no, that's fine, I promise. They'll call my cell, most likely, anyway. Listen to me – 'cell'. I sound like a local, don't I?"

I laugh. "I'm not sure you've really lost your accent, Bea."

"No. Never. I would not want to. Now, how are you and your beautiful children? And your beautiful husband?"

I had really phoned to see how she is – and Bob, of course – but something tells me she is glad of some distraction.

"Oh, we're OK, thanks, Bea. Busy as ever. But it looks like our plans for tomorrow are going to have to change."

I find myself telling her all about the weather, and the chaos it's caused. The man being swept into the waters, and the fact that the lifeboat has already been out and rescued him. I know she'll like to hear all the details, and picture how things are here. She listens intently, every now and then telling me to go on, or asking a question.

"My god, it sounds like bedlam," she says. "I don't think I've ever seen a flood like that back home."

"It really has been."

"And that poor man."

"I know."

We are quiet for a moment, then I take the plunge, and turn to the most pressing subject. Bob. "You must feel all over the place at the moment. How is he?"

"They say he's stable. But he's not conscious. They're keeping him in a coma, and with some kind of machine that's helping him breathe. I can hardly believe it."

I hadn't realised it was that bad. I feel awful for not checking in again sooner. "Oh Bea, you must feel awful." I realise I have very little idea what to say now. "I'm glad David's there with you," I try.

"Oh, me too, but he should be going home with Martin and the children. Won't hear of it, though."

That makes me smile. "That's David," I say. "And you would do exactly the same for him."

"I suppose I would."

"I'll make sure we're here for Martin when he gets back, and I'll drop off some supplies for him and the kids, too."

"That's lovely of you, Alice." I think I can hear a sob in her voice.

"It's nothing," I say. "We're all like family, aren't we? I just wish you were nearer, and I could come and see you, too. And David. This place isn't the same without you."

"I don't think I've ever felt so homesick."

"Well, when Bob's better," I say, hoping that I don't sound too flippant, "you and he had better come for a visit. Maybe a prolonged visit. You can always stop at Amethi if you want to, if we time it right."

"That sounds absolutely lovely, Alice. I think I'll take you up on that."

"Good. You just let me know, as soon as you're able."

"I will. And thank you for calling. It's lovely to hear from you, and to know that you're thinking about us. You'd better get some sleep now, my love. I'll be in touch, when there's any news."

"Any time," I say. I feel guilty for not calling her sooner. "Give my love to David."

"I will."

I hang up, trying hard to imagine what it's like for Bea at the moment. Settling down on the sofa, I rearrange myself, and Meg, who grumbles a little but then lays her head on my shoulder, sighing so that I feel her breath on my ear. I work my fingers through her thick fur, then I lay my own head down, on the cushions, and I let the night's events wash over me.

10

Some time later, in the glow of the TV, I feel a cold kiss on my cheek from Sam. Meg is no longer lying on me, no doubt having gone to greet him when he returned.

"You're back!" I say, sitting up. "How is everything? Do you want a cup of tea?"

Sam laughs quietly, "Give yourself a moment to wake up first! And I've actually possibly never had so many cups of tea in my life. I think it's the only thing people feel they can do in situations like this."

"Is it… is town a mess?"

"It's not great," he says. "But it could be worse. The pizza place, and the hairdressers, are both flooded."

"No! Diane's?" I think of the lovely woman who was so kind to Crazy Craig at the network meeting.

"Yep." Sam shakes his head. "She was inconsolable. But her son came down to get her, took her up to his place."

"Well, that's good."

"As far as I know, one of the galleries got it, too; and the newsagent, and some of the holiday places by the harbour."

"Oh, that's sad. Imagine that, when you're on holiday. You'd be paying a lot to stay in one of them, too."

"Yep… harbourside's alright, until you get a day like today. It's been even worse further up the coast, and the train line's impassable."

"Oh no!" Does that mean Sophie…"

"Yep, she's stuck, but I wouldn't want her travelling at the moment anyway."

Sam goes off to strip out of soaking wet clothes and have a hot shower, for the second time in less than twelve hours. I check my phone. I can see a message from Dad:

Festival's off, Alice. I just had word from Peter. What a night, eh?

Peter? So Dad's now got a direct line to the town mayor! Despite everything, this makes me smile. Ever since he joined the Christmas Lights committee, Dad's found more of a place for himself in the town, and it's been so good seeing him and Mum integrate, entirely independently of me and Sam.

Yep, what a night. But they rescued that man, at least.

Yes, what an idiot, eh? We are all so self-righteous, those of us who live here.

Do you know who it was?

Yes, some bloke who moved here recently. Chris, I think his name is. Got a bouncy castle company.

You don't mean Craig? An image of that larger-than-life man at the network meeting springs to mind.

That's it. Do you know him?

No, not really. I met him at the network meeting. He seems a nice bloke. I wonder what happened.

Probably just not used to living by the sea.

No, he's one of us! Midlander. Speaks like you. I feel flippant, and guilty, thinking of the nice, friendly, outgoing man. I wonder how he ended up in that situation. **Do you know if he's OK?**

Far as I know, yes. They whipped him off to get checked over, but by all accounts they found him really fast. Must have been terrifying, though. I didn't know he was from our neck of the woods. I'll have to buy him a beer.

That's a good idea. When he's recovered.

Of course.

OK... I'm going to try and get some sleep, and you should too.

I'm halfway there! Night, Alice.

Night, Dad xx

Sam is wrapped in his dressing gown, lying on the bed, looking absolutely worn out. "What a night."

"Not quite as we pictured it. There's a lot of drama round this way, isn't there?"

"It's the sea," he says. "Always poking its nose in where it's not wanted. That poor bloke, though. I didn't see him, but Andy did. Said he was in tears, and couldn't stop shaking, or thanking the crew. He kept apologising, too."

I feel a few tiny prickles on the surface of my eyes at the thought of this. I am tired, and emotional. I put my arms around Sam and hold him to me.

"Better get some sleep now," I say. "I've still got to get to work in the morning, assuming our guests can get to us. And the kids, I'm sorry to say, are not likely to let you have a lie-in."

"No, I can't see that happening, somehow."

I turn around and Sam puts his arms around me. His warmth and proximity are reassuring. I start to drift off, and something makes me catch myself, blinking my eyes against the dark of the night. The clock on the bedside table says 3:17. I have less than four hours before I have to get up again. Oh well. It's not like we'll be having that late night at the festival anymore. I will go to work for the morning, then try to get a rest in the afternoon. I don't envy Sam, being the one to tell Ben that there won't be a festival, and that his big sister won't be coming, either.

*

Up at Amethi, it is almost as if nothing has happened. The ground is carpeted with a very welcome layer of moisture, and has already greedily sucked away most of the rainfall, so that it is barely muddy at all.

Julie is already here, and I greet her with a hug. "Was Luke OK?"

"Yes, just shattered. Sam?"

"The same."

"What a nightmare."

"I know. And that poor bloke. It was that bloke I told you about – you know, Crazy Craig's Castles."

"Maybe he's crazier than you thought."

"He must be, to have let himself get that close to the waves."

"That'll put even more people's backs up – the lifeboaters having to put themselves at risk for some incomer's stupidity."

"They don't see it like that, though, at the lifeboat."

"No, but you know some people will."

That's true enough. And I do get it. If it was your partner/parent/sibling, you'd be angry at the things they have to do sometimes. And it's not just the risks they take, but the substantial disruption to their own and their families' lives. The crew were out till 4am rescuing a dog that had fallen down the cliff face the other week, despite notices asking owners to keep their dogs on leads. The knock-on effect is significant.

Our first stop is the kitchen, where Julie gets some coffee on the go. I head outside and uncover all the outdoor furniture. The sun is already well on its course for the day, making the remaining raindrops sparkle along the edges of the roof, and across the flowerheads. The birds, too, seem barely to have noticed the previous day's deluge, or perhaps are even grateful for it. Their songs flood the air, from the woods and the hedgerows and the fruit trees in the orchard.

Swallows and swifts stream across the sky, high up, screaming to each other for what seems like pure joy. I breathe long, slow, and deep. My eyes are sore with fatigue, but being here certainly takes the edge off it.

I suppose that later, even though I'd imagined resting this afternoon, I will see if there is anything we can do to help with the clear-up in town. Maybe Mum and Dad can have the kids, and Meg, and Sam and I can go down together. What a waste of all that time and effort planning our town celebration.

Still, we have houses here to vacate and clean, ready for tomorrow, and that will be a good focus for the morning. Julie and I start with the Mowhay, making sure it is clean as clean can be. There is nothing like yoga to bring your focus to how spotless (or not) a floor is.

We open the bifold doors wide, and allow the day in.

"Traitor," I scold the sunshine. "Where were you yesterday, eh?"

"I don't think the weather works like that, Alice," Julie says.

"No, well, it is very inconsiderate."

"I am more disappointed than I'd have imagined," she admits. "I think we just all needed a bit of a blow-out."

"I know. It would have been lovely."

"And now there's just going to be so much clearing up to do."

"I know. Maybe we can do it next year," I say glumly.

Lizzie appears while we're eating our breakfast; jars of overnight oats that Julie had prepared yesterday afternoon. There are little shards of crystallised ginger hidden amongst the apricots and raisins, and the sharp sweetness is just what I need.

"How are you two?" she asks. "Up all night?"

"It feels like it," I say. "Did you know what was going on?"

"No, I hadn't heard anything till just now. Slept like a baby."

She looks like she did, too. "Well, that's something!" I smile.

"Yep, but I'm going down now, see if I can help. If you don't need me here? I thought I'd set this place up tomorrow morning."

"No, that's fine. Cindy'll be here soon, so we've got it all covered, and the guests won't arrive till tomorrow afternoon, so there's loads of time. We'll probably see you later, if you're still in town."

"Lovely." She heads off into the sunshine, which lights up her frizzy hair.

"How is she always so bloody chilled… and so full of energy?" Julie grumbles good-naturedly.

"I think she's found the key to living well. She keeps trying to tell us."

"But she also only has to think about herself, doesn't have kids pestering her for snacks every five minutes, and she gets a good night's sleep every night."

"As I said, she's found the key to living well!" Actually, I know Lizzie wanted children. And she lost a baby. I am sure she'd give up her precious sleep in favour of things having turned out differently. But Julie isn't to know that.

"Well, good for her, I suppose," Julie says grudgingly, making me laugh.

"Come on," I say, "let's go for a little walk. We've got some time still before the houses are empty."

As we follow the path along the side of the field, the tall flowers brush against our clothes, the remnants of yesterday's rain creating little wet patches and seeping through to our skin. As we approach the wooded area, the birdsong takes over, and neither of us speak for a while. Without either of us suggesting it, we find our way into the bird hide, and we sit on the rough bench, with our backs against the wooden wall. In front of the hide, the branches and feeders are busy with the woodland traffic: blue tits, coal tits, goldfinches, bullfinches, tree creepers, nut hatches, wrens. All going about their business, untouched by the previous day's events.

"We should come here more often," says Julie. "We should offer birding retreats."

"With Bill Oddie?"

"Chris Packham."

"Now that would be something."

"Seriously, though, I think you're right about Lizzie having found the key. She doesn't give a shit, does she, about the small stuff? The inconsequential details that most of us spend too much time worrying about."

"I always used to think you were like that," I say. "You never seemed to be bothered about the kinds of things that stressed me out. Being late for things. Getting homework in on time. Not upsetting people."

"I was irresponsible and rude, you mean!" Julie laughs.

"Well…" I smile. "No, I don't, not really. It's hard to put my finger on it. But I've always been too keen to be polite to people, and agreeing with things they say just because it would be rude not to. You've never had a problem disagreeing with people."

"No, not when it's necessary. And sometimes it is necessary, you know. There are too many idiots out there, and if you don't challenge them, they'll happily go through life believing they're right."

"I think I just avoid confrontation wherever I can."

"I know. And that's nice, too."

"I'm not sure I want to be 'nice' anymore. I want a bit of what you've got."

"Thanks very much!" she laughs, and I do, too.

"I don't mean you're not nice! You know that. But you don't suffer fools gladly. I'm angry at people, inside. At the people who have sailed through this last year and whose prime concern is when they can go back to the pub. And I know we haven't had it bad. But at least we know that there are lots of other people who have. Sorry." I rub my eyes. "I'm just tired."

"I know. But you're right, as well. It's a weird old time we've lived through... are still living through. Let's try to make time for some of the yoga this week, OK?"

"Yes. And definitely be here for the solstice stuff."

"I feel like I need it more than ever," Julie says and, knowing how sceptical – if not cynical – she used to be, I look at my friend and see how much these last few years have changed her. She's been through the mill, with her unsuccessful attempts at pregnancy, and the tough, rigorous process of adoption. But she's risen to every challenge, and I am awed by her strength and resilience. I am tearful again, and I need to pull myself together before she notices.

But she puts her hand on mine, without looking at me. "I know," she says.

11

"Are we still going to the festival, Mummy?" asks Ben, as we walk down the hill towards town. He is holding onto me with one hand and grasping the flag he made with the other.

"It's not happening anymore, Ben," I say. I know Sam has already told him this, but I think he does not want to believe it.

"They'll have to have it another time," Sam says, "because of the weather."

"But it's sunny!" Ben protests, his face threatening tears.

He's got a point. After yesterday's onslaught, today has dawned as any festival day should. Vivid, clear skies, and a cheerful sun. The breeze is still fresh, however, making garden flowers dance, and sending litter skittering along the streets.

"I know, it's nice now. But it rained so much, and the tide came in, and it soaked everything. They can't operate the fair because the ground's too muddy, and some of the buildings have been flooded, too," Sam explains. He's got Holly in the backpack and she's holding his hair with both hands, grinning away merrily. It makes no odds to her whether the festival is happening or not. She's just glad to be out, with her family, and she's even more delighted when we go up the steps to the Sail Loft. She starts bouncing up and down with excitement. Meg trots obediently at Sam's side, also just happy to be out.

We pass a couple of Mum and Dad's guests, who are on

their way down the hotel steps. They smile at us. "Bit damp yesterday, eh?" the man smiles.

"Just a bit! It's a shame for your holiday."

"Oh, it didn't bother us. We just stayed in our room, reading, and watching the sea from our window. Somebody said they had the lifeboat out, though."

"Yes, I heard that," I say, wondering how Craig is.

"Damn silly, getting too close to the sea like that."

"Definitely," says Sam. "There's always one or two, though – seems like fun, till you get caught off-guard by a huge wave, or lose your footing."

"Well, I suppose if you're not from the coast, you don't always get it," I say. I feel protective of Craig for some reason. "I don't suppose he meant to get washed out to sea."

The couple look like they want to get on their way.

"Anyway, have a lovely day today," I say. "You might want to stay up in the high town, although I imagine the clean-up is already going on. We're just going to leave these three here, then we'll be going to help, ourselves."

"Oh, are you Sue and Phil's daughter?" the woman asks. "We've heard so much about you, and especially you two," she offers a dimpled smile to Ben and Holly. "Did you make that flag yourself?" she asks Ben.

"Yes," he says, his chest puffing out proudly.

"Well, it's lovely. Be good for your granny and grandpa, and maybe we'll see you later."

"Bye," says Ben, and Holly echoes him, waving from her lofty seat as the couple disappear off down the hill.

Mum and Dad are full of news and opinions on what's been happening.

"The school's open, as planned, but the shows are

cancelled, of course," says Dad. "They're still doing food and drink, for everyone involved in the clean-up, and the buses are still free, so people can get up and down town easily, and have a break at the school before heading back."

"They opened last night, for the people whose holiday lets flooded - apparently some of the classrooms have got beds in them, and lots of people have taken up sleeping bags and pillows – far too many, by the sound of things!" Mum adds. "Isn't it nice that everyone's pulling together?"

It is, I think. And even though we're all a bit downhearted that the festival's been cancelled, I have a warm feeling at the thought of so many people helping to make things better.

"Sounds like that bloke's back home now," says Dad. "They checked him over and he was alright, just a bit shaken up."

"Good," says Sam. "Hopefully he won't do anything so stupid again."

"Sam!" I say. I am a bit surprised by how sharp he's being, particularly given his own accident not so long ago. He's lived here all his life, so is far from ignorant of the dangers. Yet he still went off up the cliffs that night, and had a fall which might easily have killed him.

"Well…" he says.

"Well nothing! We all do stupid things sometimes."

"I guess."

I suppose the problem is that we are all feeling stressed and anxious. And Sam knows the guys on the lifeboat pretty well. Perhaps he also feels some guilt for his own accident. Even so, his attitude is grating on me.

"Come on," I say. "Let's go and do something positive."

Sam manages to extricate himself from the backpack, and

places it on the floor, Holly wriggling and desperate to get out. Ben has already dashed into the lounge, where he's put the TV on and is expertly zooming through the channels to find CBeebies. I unfasten Holly and give her a cuddle.

"She's due a nap," I tell Mum, "but she's also very excited, so it might be a while before she goes off."

"Don't you worry, she'll be fine. Ben, too. Go on, off you go. And let me know if we can help with anything."

"We will. Thank you, Mum." I kiss her and Holly, then Dad and Ben, who are both now watching *Hey Duggee*, Meg settled on the seat next to Dad. Then Sam and I head out to find out what's going on, and how we might be of use.

As we walk down the hill, Sam takes my hand. This small gesture somehow removes all traces of tension between us. I look at him and smile.

"It's like old times, isn't it?" he says, and I am transported back a decade or two. The few dates we had that first summer we met, when we'd finally got it together, and he would meet me after work so we could head down to town or, more often, the beach. The elation of walking hand-in-hand with him back then. The feeling that life was opening up before us, and I couldn't even see the horizon. Everything was ours for the taking.

These days, some of that empty space has been filled, and mostly by great things: Sam and the children; Amethi; Mum and Dad; the extended family I have here in Cornwall these days, with Julie, Luke and Zinnia top of that list. I must think of this when I'm feeling low. All that hope that I had, when I was eighteen – well, maybe things haven't quite panned out exactly as I'd imagined they would back then, but to my mind they've been even better. If Sam and I had not lost touch initially, our relationship might have fizzled out. It is true that I would never have met or gone out with Geoff, of course, but despite the fact that our relationship was so unhealthy, and he made me so unhappy, I know I learned a lot from it. Also, Sam would not have got together with Kate, and there would be no Sophie (well, not in our lives, anyway), which is unthinkable. If Mum had not had her heart problems, perhaps she and Dad would still be five hours' drive up country. Each little twist of fate has brought me to where I am today, and who knows where a twist in a different direction may have landed me?

As we turn onto the street where I used to live, back when I rented from David, I stop Sam for just a moment, and I place my hands on his shoulders. "I love you," I say, kissing him on the mouth.

"I love you too," he says, looking surprised and pleased.

"I don't think I say it as much as I used to. But I mean it more than ever."

"I know exactly what you mean." He kisses me softly, then more firmly, then he pulls me to him. "We don't do this enough, either."

"I know. It's a bit difficult, or different at the very least, these days."

"Let's try and make it less difficult, shall we?"

"It's a deal."

"But right now, we'd better get to town," he says, and he puts his arm round me, so that we walk close together, and into the centre of last night's disaster. And I know disaster is a strong word. It's not like it was an earthquake like they had last year in Greece and Turkey, or a flood on the scale of those we've seen in countries like India and Bangladesh.

But for those people whose business premises have been flooded, and anyone whose home or holiday let has suffered the same fate, it has been disastrous. It seems that it was a combination of factors all coming together to cause the problems. The heavy rain ("Apparently a month's worth fell over four hours," claims Bella, from the bakers up the hill) hitting the past-its-best drainage system ("I've been pushing the council to do something about this for bloody years," huffs Harry Turner, one of Dad's mates), combined with the flow of water coming down from high up the town, and then the high tide ("I said this was coming," says Caleb from Dough Nuts, the pizza shop, who is busy slopping buckets of water out of his premises). Each one of these factors taken alone, the town may have been able to withstand, but combined, it was too much.

The streets now are damp, and water has pooled in places, but the heat of the day is helping to dry them out. Looking ahead, there is even visible condensation rising, as the excess moisture is drawn into the air. However, though the water is less of a presence (the sea is keeping a discreet distance now, too, like a dog that knows it's misbehaved), there are signs everywhere of the previous night's problems. Litter is strewn along the streets and pavements – washed out of bins and recycling boxes and bags, which themselves were lifted by the water or the wind, and deposited far from home. There is litter from the sea as well: seaweed, and driftwood, and sand. We find Ron down on the harbour, typically in the centre of things. He greets us with a smile and a hug for me, and a slap on the back for Sam.

"Come to help, I see! Good on you. Kids with Karen?"

"No, we dropped them at the Sail Loft," I say, guiltily.

"Of course, of course," Ron just smiles. "Well, look, let's see what we can get you doing, shall we? I think we've got a lot of things covered, but there's a load of bins that need taking back to where they came from. Some of them have got addresses on, so that's easy enough, but maybe you can nip along and give people a knock – see what they're missing, eh? They're already doing the streets that way, so maybe you can head along towards the station and start there? Make a list and we'll try and redistribute them. Not very exciting, I know, sorry."

"We're not here for excitement, Ron," I smile. "Such a shame about the festival, though."

"I know, I know. We'll have to think again about that, but first we need to get things back to how they were. There's businesses and holidays that need rescuing."

I like the way he's thinking of the holidays as well. There are a lot of people round here who would put them at the bottom of the list – especially where the holiday lets are owned by people out of town – but for each damaged property, there is loss of income, not just for the letting agent or owner, but for local businesses, too; there is also the disappointment of a cancelled holiday, and I really do appreciate how important a week or two here is to so many people.

It's nice to be paired with Sam, and we decide to walk as far as we can along the affected streets. We knock on doors and are by and large greeted by friendly faces. There are still some windows with signs saying the person inside is shielding – keeping themselves in isolation to try and avoid covid, normally because of other health concerns. We decide to leave these people alone, and try to work out what they might be missing by process of elimination.

After an hour or so, we return to find Ron and hand over the information we've gleaned so far.

"Great work, kids," he says. Why do I like being called a kid so much? Because it's unlikely to happen for much longer, I suspect. "Go and get yourselves up to the school for a bite to eat and a drink, then report back to me! Go on, it's not often you'll get a free bus ride!"

"Well, if you insist," I say.

Sam and I join a short queue of people and it's not long before the bus arrives. We clamber on, and sit at the back. Sam puts his arm around me, and it makes me giggle. I know I shouldn't be enjoying this so much, but somehow it's turned into a really fun afternoon. Better still, when we get to the school, we hear loud music coming from inside.

Mrs Taylor, the headteacher, is greeting people. "Hello!" she says. "Welcome. As you can hear, the bands have decided to play on. I don't wish to make any comparisons to the Titanic…!" she grins.

"This is great," I say. "How lovely to have music."

"It is, it is," she agrees, "although you will note I've brought myself out here for a little while. It's brightened up the experience for the volunteers, though. And we'll be keeping the doors open tonight, as planned, for a bit of a get together. We might not be able to have a festival, but with everything set up in here, it seems a shame not to use it."

"I heard you had people sleeping up here, too."

"Yes, well, just last night. All the holiday makers have gone home now, poor things, and the few people whose own homes were flooded have been found rooms at the hotels and B&Bs."

"That's great," says Sam.

"Yes, isn't it? Makes you very proud of this community."
"It really does."

With so many people helping out, the town is looking almost back to its normal self by late evening. The affected premises need specialist help, of course, and there are also hygiene issues, as who knows what the flood waters have brought in with them, so these are left alone by the majority of us. There are some immediate tasks to be carried out, including throwing away food and soft furnishings where applicable (after taking photos for the insurance claims). It's a sad sight, seeing people clearing things out, and it must be incredibly stressful, but there is a general feeling of good cheer.

Peter Oswald, the mayor, has elected to speak to us all at the harbourside. "I just want to thank all of you for volunteering and getting stuck in today," he says. "I know it's been a huge disappointment for us all, not to be able to go ahead with our celebration as planned, but we will regroup, and the festival will go ahead another time. Right now, the immediate focus has to be on getting the town back to normal, and helping our fellow residents and business owners get back on their feet. To that effect, with the blessing of the town council and, I hope, all the people who have been kind enough to donate prizes, we are still going to be drawing the names for the raffle. The proceeds will go towards helping people who need it to recover from the floodwater."

There is general cheering at this.

"What about putting it towards new drainage for the town?" somebody shouts, and there is a ripple of laughter.

"Yes, well, that is a matter for the county council, but believe me, we will be putting some pressure on them in the light of these events, we cannot delay any longer. We can't see this happen again. You can all help, by writing to the council, and the MP, too. Let them see how much we want and need this. Now, it's getting on, and there's not a lot more we can do here today. I hope to see many of you up at the school, where we'll be treated to performances by some of our best local bands. Go and let your hair down. Enjoy yourselves. You deserve it."

There is a round of applause, and I feel a little shiver of goose pimples run across me. It may sound cheesy, but today has ended up being a special day for the town despite everything, and we've achieved one of the aims of the festival – after all the unpleasantness and isolation and sometimes divisiveness of the pandemic, we had wanted to bring people back together.

12

Sam and I wake up on Sunday morning, both with slightly sore heads. On our way up to the school yesterday evening, I had called Mum and Dad and asked if it would be OK for Ben and Holly and Meg to stay the night with them.

"Great minds think alike!" Mum said. "I was just about to suggest that. We've got Carly in to waitress in the morning so I can stop up here with the kiddies, while your dad cooks breakfast."

I gave Sam a thumbs-up, and he grinned. Suddenly, we were having a night out, just the two of us. OK, maybe it was in the primary school hall, but I'll take what I can get these days. Besides, there was live music, Julie and Luke were there, and a load of other people we knew, and everyone was in the mood to have some fun.

The bar was well stocked, and exceedingly cheap. I drank a lot more than I have in some time, but I just felt like letting go a bit. For once, not thinking about the children, or work, or my never-ending to-do list. I did feel slightly guilty that we were out partying while some people were struggling with ruined businesses, but Diane the hairdresser was there, and putting away the pre-mixed gin & tonics, and later I saw Caleb from the pizza place with his wife, Ilyana. I groan as I remember talking to them, for quite a long time, and possibly labouring the point about how sorry I was about the flood but what a great place the town is, and what a sense of community there is. I am sure they smiled politely throughout, no doubt wishing I'd shut up about it all.

Diane, as well, I must have made a beeline for, but at least we know each other relatively well. "I'm just so sorry," I seem to remember slurring at her, and her kind, benign smile. She's a neat, petite woman, and I always feel a bit like a scruffy giant next to her.

"Thank you, Alice," she had put her hand on my arm. "But it's just a building. Think of that poor man who nearly drowned."

"Ah, yes, the bouncy castle guy. Do you know how he is?"

"I haven't heard anything since this morning. I'm going to keep an eye out for when he's back home. I don't suppose he's had a chance to build up much support round here, yet."

"You are an angel, Diane," I'd said, and… had I hugged her? Yes, I seem to remember pulling her in for a great big cuddle, her face pressed probably uncomfortably somewhere near my chest. I groan.

"You OK?" Sam asks, propping himself up on his elbow.

"Yeah, just remembering my drunken exuberance last night."

"You weren't too bad," he smiles. "Just… happy. Friendly."

"Over-friendly?"

"Well…"

"I'll take that as a yes."

"I think it's endearing."

"You're biased."

He goes to kiss me, but I roll away. "I didn't brush my teeth last night. Let me go and do that. I'll be back."

I feel ever so slightly light-headed as I get out of bed, but I go through to the bathroom, brush my teeth and splash water on my face, and I feel a bit more human. Returning to bed, I take a big gulp of water from the glass on the bedside table, then I lie down next to Sam.

"Ready?" he smiles.

"Ready."

He goes to kiss me again, and I close my eyes. His kiss is so very, very gentle that at first I barely feel it, but then his teeth graze my lips, and I find myself moving closer to him, pressing myself against him. All thoughts of sore heads and embarrassing drunken behaviour slide clean away. With no kids, and not even Meg, in the house, we need to make the most of this very precious time to ourselves. In the lazy, hazy Sunday morning sunlight that filters in through the curtains, we do just that.

Later, we take a walk down to town. The damaged properties are open to the elements; the sunshine and heat have returned with a vengeance, which will help the drying efforts, and which also make it feel like nothing untoward has happened. The new tranche of holiday-makers has arrived, having missed the drama of Friday, and to all intents and purposes, much of town is as it should be.

I've said we'd collect the kids after lunch, so we have some time to ourselves. We treat ourselves to a coffee at the Beach Bar, where our friends Andy and Becky, who run the bar, and whose son Zach is the same age as Ben, are also nursing hangovers, then we walk up behind the beach and along the cliff path a little way, stopping at a patch of rocks, where we sit, soaking up the sun, and looking out to sea. We are not all that far from where Sam fell down the cliff, and the thought makes me wince, as it often does. When he'd recovered from his injuries, he'd insisted we came for a walk up here, so that we didn't avoid it and associate it with bad memories. He doesn't like to talk about that night, although he did once tell me how scared he had been. I think he just wants to forget it ever happened. I wonder how Craig is feeling now; I imagine that relief and gratitude at being rescued can turn into something darker – the 'what ifs'.

I scan the sea now, as ever looking for dolphins, but can only see seabirds at the moment. Not that they are 'only' seabirds. I love them, but I can't deny there is something just a little bit more magical in the sight of a pod of dolphins cutting across the bay.

The rocks are warm against my back, and I close my eyes, resting my head against Sam's shoulder. If I'm not careful, I'll fall asleep. This is the most relaxed I have felt for some time, and I could stay here all day. I know I can't, and maybe that makes this half an hour or so all the more special.

I consider how this town – which once was a place that seemed to me to exist only in my mind, once I'd gone back home and the summer was long past, and it seemed almost unreal to think that just a few hours away were the beaches, and the sea, and the tides trekking in and out – is now home. And how, with living here, it has borne witness to so many of my life events, both good and bad. There are so many places now which hold special significance, and I visualise a map highlighting them. The trauma of Sam's fall should be marked by a scar; the wound has healed, but its effects will never be completely gone. The rock where I met Sophie – I would mark this with a bucket, or a crab, signifying the moment she sloshed her rockpool water over me (accidentally, I might add). David's old house; the Sail Loft;

the beach where Sam and I first met, and where I saw him again ten years later; our house; Julie and Luke's house; even Joe's café. And of course Amethi, which holds so many different memories, from the horrible encounter with the unstable Tony a few years back to Sam's surprise 'wedding' ceremony, and Holly's birth. I suppose this is the difference between loving a place where you live, and loving a place from afar. Back then, after just one summer, I knew I loved it here, and I knew I wanted to be here, but it was superficial, really. Maybe that's not fair – I had a genuine draw to it, and not just because of Sam. But now, I feel like my life is woven into the fabric of the place, along with so many thousands of others over the years.

Not all that far from where we are sitting is another key place to highlight on my map: the little old hut, where Sam and I once sheltered from a storm so many years ago. The romance of that moment! I remember feeling so wrapped up in our relationship, like it was the most important thing in the world. I couldn't stop thinking about Sam, including when I got back home, and went on to uni. When I look at the little hut now, I don't think I would dare go inside, for fear of it collapsing. Probably it ought to be dismantled or made safe, but so far it has been left, and for much of the year it is well-hidden by overgrown brambles and gorse. Maybe it was less dilapidated back then; I suppose it was nearly twenty years ago. But maybe we just didn't think in the same way – seeing and assessing dangers and risks everywhere. Something that comes with being a parent, perhaps, or maybe it's just getting older that makes you feel a little less indestructible; probably it's a bit of both.

We walk back to town hand-in-hand, passed occasionally by other walkers, who nod and smile and wish us a pleasant walk. A harassed-looking family come by, with three children, the youngest of whom is in tears. "I understand," I want to say, thinking that Sam and I probably look like we don't have a care in the world. But I just smile and try to convey my sympathy with my eyes.

I love seeing the town swing into view as we round the corner of the headland. I don't think I will ever tire of this sight. With the sun at its peak in the sky, and against a backdrop of the bluest of skies, the buildings and beaches are really showing themselves off to their best advantage, as though fully aware of their effect on the incomers, some of whom may be arriving here for the first ever time; others drawn back year after year, needing a dose of this place to keep them going. Windows shine, gulls cry, and the sea twinkles and dimples prettily. I stop for a second, and get Sam to do the same.

"Just look," I say. "That's where we live."

"It is."

"Well, we must be some of the luckiest people alive."

"I suppose you're right." Having spent all of his life here, Sam doesn't always appreciate it quite as much as I do, or at least not in the same way. To live by the sea is perfectly normal to him. To me, even after all these years, it feels like I've won first prize.

We walk on again, in companionable silence. The air hums with insects, and sparrows tweet and chatter and flutter about in amongst a tangle of brambles and wild roses. A tiny lizard scurries across the path in front of us. Full summer is upon us, and already it feels like the festival that never was is a thing of the past. A disappointment, but one which has been quickly overcome.

Back in town, we are sweating by the time we get to the Sail Loft, and Mum ushers us in for a cold drink and a seat on the veranda. My mind begins to turn to work, and the solstice retreat. We decline Dad's offer of lunch, and take the kids home, where we have sandwiches and cans of pop in the back garden, and fill the little paddling pool, covering it with a gazebo.

"I'd better get up to Amethi soon," I say to Sam, "if you don't mind."

"Of course. You go. It's been lovely, though." He takes my hand and smiles, and kisses me.

"It has."

I kiss the kids goodbye, and promise to be back in time for tea. "Why don't we invite Karen and Ron?" I say to Sam.

"Er, yeah, we could do," he says.

"Go on, let's." There is a very slight niggle in my mind left over from Ron asking if we'd left the kids with Karen yesterday – if I'm honest, it hadn't even crossed my mind, and I feel a bit guilty that my mum and dad are my default childcare option – and I am keen to put as many things right as I possibly can.

"Yeah!" shouts Ben, splashing water into the air. "Granny and Ron!"

"That's Grandad Ron to you, you cheeky monkey," I say. "Go on, Sam, see if they'd like to come. We can get some fish & chips or something."

"Alright," Sam smiles. "If you insist."

"I do."

I drive up to Amethi, feeling happier than I have in some

time, and I wouldn't really say I've been unhappy. But now, the car windows down, the town and sea behind me and the promise of a long, hot summer ahead, I laugh out loud, at just how very good life can be. Meg, in the boot, probably thinks I'm mad, but I can see her face as she's sitting up, peering over the back seat, the wind in her fur, and I could swear that she is smiling, too.

All our yoga guests arrive on time, with no hiccups, and are greeted warmly by Lizzie, who has spent the morning dressing the Mowhay beautifully, with flowers from the meadows, and the battery-powered candles and lanterns, to provide soft lighting for late evening and early morning practice. Julie arrives to an enthusiastic greeting from Meg, who then returns to a cool spot in the shade. When everyone is gathered together, Lizzie introduces herself, and then me and Julie.

"Welcome, everyone. I am so happy to have you here, to celebrate the solstice, and spend a few days focusing on yourselves. It isn't selfish; well, not in a bad way! I believe it's a necessity, and after these few days for yourselves, I hope you can return to your homes, your jobs, your families, refreshed and recharged. It's been a hard time for many of us, and I'd like this week for us to focus on ourselves and healing, and positivity. We are celebrating the solstice and this special day of light. This is the start of true summer, and a time to remember that there is hope in the world, which seems perhaps more important now than ever. But we will get further into that tomorrow. For now, I'll just tell you a little about the next few days, and remind you that this time really is for you, and I hope you can make the most of it."

She gives a brief run-down of the plan for the week, and then asks if Julie or I would like to say a few words.

I go first: "I'd just like to welcome all of you to Amethi. I know some of you have been here before, more than once, and for some of you it's your first time. All I can say is, Lizzie is a wonderful yoga teacher, and has put a lot of effort into planning this week. You also have the benefit of some delicious, healthy food cooked by Julie, who can tell you a bit about that. And don't worry, it may be healthy, but I am sure she'll be throwing in a few treats, too. I'll be heading off home soon, but I will be here bright and early in the morning to celebrate the solstice with you all, and I can't wait. It is always an extra special day, and a highlight of our year here."

"Thanks, Alice," says Julie. "I can't say I have a lot to add to that! But I will speak to you all separately about the menu, to make sure I've got all your dietary requirements right. Usually, we have a feast to celebrate the solstice, but this year we'll do it a bit differently and there will be a last-night party, when you can eat and drink and be merry. We don't want you to peak too soon tomorrow, and not be able to make the most of your yoga sessions!"

As Julie sits down next to me, the room lights up with conversation, and happy voices. It is such a pleasure, and I have missed this very much, being able to host social events like this. I stay for a cup of Lizzie's solstice tea, made with rose petals, spearmint, lemongrass and lemon balm, and then I say my goodbyes, and I head off home.

*

"Hello!" I call as I walk into the cool hallway, hearing voices from the garden. Meg dashes past me, having heard Ron's voice. She loves everyone, but there are certain people she really can't get enough of, and Ron is one of them. I step outside to see her trying to clamber onto him while he laughingly gives her a hand up.

"Get down, Meg," I scold, but I already know there is no reasoning with her, or with Ron. The feeling definitely goes both ways with these two.

"Hi, Alice," Karen stands to give me a hug and a kiss, and both Holly and Ben run up to join in. "Sam's gone down to the chippy, he said he'll be back soon."

"Brilliant, I am really hungry."

"Probably a delayed hangover!" Karen says. "I heard last night was a good one."

"It really was. You should have been there."

"I know. Ron was so tired, though."

"I'm not surprised. It must have been a long day."

"Ah well, I don't mind," Ron says. "It was worth it. I'm just glad things weren't worse."

"I know. Such a shame."

"But we don't stop for anything, or anyone, down here. We're already looking for another date for the festival."

"Really?"

"Yes! Course. Can't have all that planning for nothing, can we? We'll work something out."

"That would be great." I don't know how much I mean that; I can't see it, somehow. Maybe the moment has passed. I won't say that, though.

Sam soon returns, with enough fish and chips to feed an army. I don't even eat fish, so I have some of the chips, and get a couple of slices of bread. "Can't beat a chip butty!"

"Is that what they're having up at Amethi?" Sam grins.

"Erm, no, I think it's curry and brown rice."

"Ha!"

We sit outside until the sun has passed our garden and it's time for the children to go to bed. Karen and Ron stay on, and we sit in the lounge with the French doors open, and Sam opens a bottle of wine. I only have a small glass, and I keep half an eye on the time, as I know I need to be up early. It feels nice, though, to spend this time with Sam's mum, and Sam seems relaxed and happy. He is talking with Ron about something to do with the lifeboat, when Karen turns to me.

"Alice," she says, in such a way that I feel a small sense of dread creeping in.

"Yes?"

"You know I missed last night's shenanigans?"

"At the school? It was hardly shenanigans," I say cautiously, wondering where this is going.

"Well, it got me thinking, I miss nights out. I mean, I'm happy with Ron, of course I am. Happier than I've ever been. But he's not really what you might call wild," she says conspiratorially. "And I've decided that, before I marry him, and settle down for good, I want a proper hen do."

"Really?" I ask.

I'd pictured a nice little meal somewhere local – probably the Cross-Section – followed by drinks, and back home and in bed by midnight.

"Yes! And I know exactly where. Newquay!" she grins. "The capital of stag and hen parties... well, without going abroad. And I want you and Julie to organise it!"

13

Thoughts of a wild night in Newquay are so at odds with the solstice retreat, I have to put them out of my head, and decide I'll come back to that subject next weekend, after the retreat, and after Ben's birthday, too. Maybe Karen will change her mind, anyway. I do not even mention it to Julie. The problem is, I think she might love the idea. It will appeal to her sense of mischief.

Julie and I arrive at Amethi in the near-darkness, and find everyone gathered around the fire that Lizzie has got going. She is in her standard poncho, while everyone else is wearing fleeces and hoodies, and even dry robes. The air is not yet warm, perhaps holding a little of the dampness from Friday's rain, so the heat of the fire is much appreciated.

Lizzie has more solstice tea on the go, and she guides us through a few basic yoga moves to keep us warm while we await the rising of the sun. I catch Julie yawning, and think we should really have stayed overnight up here, but it's harder to do things like that when you've got children to think about. And so we shared a lift, the stars looking down on us before the light began gradually to grow, and they faded back into the unknown.

As we stepped out of the car into the car park, trying our best to keep quiet, even though everyone who is staying there was already awake, we heard an owl calling from the line of trees, and we both stopped still. Julie grasped my hand and we smiled at each other, like a pair of excited school children.

There is something about being up at that time of day, when you know most people are still asleep. Animals, too. Meg was not getting up for anybody this morning – I had a cursory wag of the tail, and that was it.

Another owl returned the call, and it sent a thrill through me. We walked together, still holding hands, towards the crackling of the fire and the murmuring voices, dropping each other's hands as we approached, although I don't suppose any of these people would have batted an eyelid.

The first time we had a solstice celebration, I was not sure how it would work. I didn't know Lizzie all that well, and I wasn't sure what I would make of the whole pagan kind of celebration, but it moved me, and I remember being surprised by how into it Julie was, too. Today is no different, and as Lizzie guides us all gently through the rituals, I find myself once more with tears in my eyes. She speaks for a while, and I listen to her warm voice, her round vowels softening the words. Looking around the group, seeing faces illuminated by the light of the flames, it is clear we are all somewhat mesmerised. We want to hear what Lizzie is saying. We want to feel the positivity she is trying to pass to us: "The cycle of our lives is represented by the cycle of the sun and, just as we align with the moon's journey every month, we can align with the sun's journey throughout the year. Each solstice and each equinox represents something different: the summer solstice is a reminder to look within, and seek the nourishment we need to grow and evolve. We pause, and wait for the energy planted in the spring to bloom. This is a time for patience, to develop trust and confidence in ourselves, in what we set in motion previously, even if we go through some troubled times. During the long days of summer, the sun provides nourishment – to the plants and trees, and the crops that we grow, and to our spirits, for the continual journey we travel from darkness to light. Summer reminds us that there is hope in the world; it is a time to seek and find meaning in our journey, even when things seem uncertain. Like the sun, we will rise each day, no matter what life brings us."

There was a part of me that might have found such a speech almost embarrassing in the past; I'd have tried to make light of it, not sure where I stood with all the hippy stuff, as Ron calls it. But over these last few years, I've become increasingly convinced by Lizzie's outlook on life. Surrounded by like-minded people, I let her words sink in, and I roll my shoulders back and look to the east, where, sure enough, the sun is beginning to take control of the sky. We welcome the spirits, and as in previous years, we write down our wishes, casting them to the flames and letting them rise into the new day.

As we go inside the Mowhay for breakfast, most of us stay quiet and thoughtful, enjoying warm, fresh bread and local butter and preserves, yoghurt and muesli. A far cry from last night's chip butty.

Later, Lizzie and our guests enjoy a day of peaceful, slow and gentle yoga, incorporating a siesta after lunch, and time in the gardens and grounds.

Julie and I have work to do, but manage to join the afternoon yoga session, then it's back to the office for me, and the kitchen for Julie. I stay on for a dinner of roasted aubergine and red pepper rice with crispy satay tofu and kale and tangy pickled cucumber, followed by butterscotch mascarpone, strawberries and meringues.

At the end of a long, peaceful day, Julie and I head back home together, the town and the sea spreading out before us, and the promise of family time, and comfortable beds, where we can rest and let the world settle around us.

14

On Thursday, the guests all leave, offering thanks and promises to come again. And then there is peace once more. I do love these occasional weeks when we've hosted a yoga or a writing event, and are treated to a couple of days with the place to ourselves. It's a break from the constant tide of holidaymakers, and on a practical level, it's a chance to get any repairs or paint jobs done on the holiday lets. On a deeper level, it's an opportunity to really rest, knowing there is nobody to ask for a hand booking a taxi, or a dinner reservation, or a last-minute change of menu for Julie. And while generally our self-catering guests keep themselves to themselves, and appreciate the peace and tranquillity as much as we do, Amethi really does take on a different ambience when there is nobody staying here.

The birds, which are relatively tame anyway, seem even braver, coming to peck crumbs from the tables outside the Mowhay, even while we are sitting there. And I feel brave enough to bring my laptop outside for a while to work, knowing that I am unlikely to be interrupted.

Lizzie is around somewhere, but I think the retreats take it out of her, so she's happy to just chill in the cottage, or sometimes she goes and hangs out in the bird hide.

Meg also seems more relaxed, and just trots about the place, or on a hot day like today she lolls around in the shade.

Today is extra-special, though, and this beautiful peace and quiet will be punctured and deflated this afternoon, when Ben and his friends arrive. For today is my little boy's birthday, and he is going to be a whole four years old. Which means that his world is going to change in a couple of months, when he 'graduates' from nursery and begins his time at school. He seems too little for school – and I'm not sure I'm ready for it, but I suspect he is.

Still, we wanted to do something special for the last of his 'baby' birthdays (don't tell him I called them that – Ben is very sure that he is not, and never has been, a baby). And the timing is perfect; with Amethi being free of guests, we have a ready-made venue, and an amazing chef at our disposal. Not put off by the fact that on Wednesday she cooked up a huge feast for the end of the yoga retreat, Julie is all abuzz with ideas for Ben's birthday party food, for children and adults, and while she's run some ideas past me, I'm happy to let her go with it. I've booked a children's entertainer for a magic show, and party games, which is great, as I dread having to run a party and organise games – sending tearful kids back to their seats because they've wobbled in Musical Statues, and having to adjudicate an argument about whose bum was first on the last chair in Musical Chairs. I am wrapped up with filling party bags and have been determined to be original, not just give the kids a load of plastic tat that will gather dust in their houses. It turns out that's harder than it sounds. In the end I've gone for a box of raisins (healthy), a Kinder bar, a pencil, a rubber, a small notepad, and a little grow-your-own veg kit.

Sam is planning to come up to Amethi after lunch, then he'll go and get Ben and Holly from nursery and bring them up here. The party starts at four, and there will be younger and older siblings as well as Ben's friends. I feel far more excited and nervous than I should.

At ten past twelve, the entertainer phones me. "Is that Ben's mum?"

"Yes, speaking."

"It's Seb here. I am really sorry to do this, but I've got covid. I just got my result back. I am so sorry."

"Oh no." My first thought is for Ben's party, but I remember my manners. "I'm so sorry to hear that. I hope you're OK."

"Not great, to be honest. I've got a bad sore throat and my head's throbbing—"

I don't have time to listen to Seb's ailments. "Well, I hope you feel better soon. Make sure you rest up. Thank you for letting me know."

"I am so sorry," he says again.

"Don't worry. It can't be helped."

Damn. What can I do now? I really, really don't want to do party games. I call Sam.

"How about a bouncy castle?" he asks.

"Oh, I don't know…"

"Why not? There's plenty of space."

"I guess. But could we get one at the last minute?"

"We can try. Look, I'm on my way up now. If you Google some numbers, we can call around and see what we can do."

"If we can't, you're going to have to wrap up one huge pass-the-parcel."

"Sure," he laughs.

"And do egg and spoon races."

"I'm on it."

At least we have the blessing of the weather. It's warm, and a little overcast today, which is better than full-on sunshine, and the risk of sunburned children and adults. We can have the Mowhay doors open, and there's so much space for the kids to go wild in. And at this age, children's parents tend to stick around, so thankfully I won't have the responsibility for looking after fifteen four-year-olds, not to mention their brothers and sisters.

By the time Sam arrives, I have a list of numbers and we try them all, but predictably it is too last-minute. There are so many events at this time of year, we really ought to have booked well in advance.

"There is one other option…" I say. "Craig. You know, the new guy."

"The one who nearly drowned?"

"Yes. I know. It's a bit soon, isn't it? I heard he was back home now, but maybe he won't want to be disturbed."

"Have you got a number for him?"

"No, but we must be able to get hold of one."

I think I know who to try first.

"Cut'n'Di hair salon," Diane's voice trills. "How can I help you?"

"Hi, Diane. It's Alice, up at Amethi."

"Oh, Alice, hi, how are you?"

"I'm fine thanks." I feel the need to move the conversation on with minimal small talk, though it feels a bit rude. "I'm really sorry to bother you; I know how busy you must be getting everything back in order. But do you by any chance have a number for Craig Cash?"

"I certainly do. May I ask what it's about?"

"Erm…" She sounds like she's his PA, screening calls for

him. "It's our Ben's birthday, actually, and the entertainer we booked has got covid. So I wondered if there was any chance Craig is well enough, and available, to set up a bouncy castle up here at Amethi? Today," I laugh nervously.

"Oh, well, I am sure he'd love to hear from you, Alice. Sorry if I sounded a bit abrupt, he's just having a tough time recovering from… everything…"

"I'm sorry to hear that," I say, and I feel like I should ask more, but the urgency of the situation here is pressing on me. "If you can let me have his number, please, you would be a life-saver. We've got about twenty kids turning up this afternoon, and no way of entertaining them!"

"Of course."

I ring Craig and explain who I am, and what the situation is. "But I know you might be still recovering from … your accident … so no pressure," I say.

"Oh, don't you worry about that. I am delighted to hear from you, Alice. I remember you from the meeting, you're the fellow Midlander, aren't you?"

"That's right," I smile.

"Well, how much space have you got?"

"Quite a bit," I muse, "but a lot of it's wildflower meadow."

"Well, we don't want to ruin that, do we? But I do need to make sure there are places where we can secure the castle to keep everything safe. Can you give me your address, Alice, and I'll come up and have a look. See what I can do."

"Oh, would you? Thank you so much, Craig."

"My pleasure, honestly."

I tell him how to get to Amethi, then Sam and I put the finishing touches to party bags, counting and double-counting to make sure that every child has one, and then

Craig arrives. He's wearing another bright shirt, and he rounds the corner, giving us his expansive smile.

"Hi Craig," I say. "Thank you so much for doing this. This is my husband, Sam."

"Hi, Sam." They shake hands. "Now, let's see how we can make your little boy's birthday party the best he's ever had, shall we?"

"He's not really had one before. He's only four," I say.

"So it should be easy enough to make sure it's the best!" Sam grins.

Craig is looking around us. "What about… over there?" he gestures towards the space outside the Mowhay. "Does that furniture move?"

"It certainly does."

"Great, well I reckon I've just the size for that space. Can I just measure up?"

"Of course."

We walk across and when he sees the Mowhay itself, his eyes light up. "This is some place!"

"Thank you," I say. "We use that space for parties, and yoga retreats, and writing courses."

"I've got a little indoor castle, too. Great for little ones."

"Have you really?"

"Yes. I can bring that. We can have one outdoors, with a slide attachment, and a little one inside."

"That sounds perfect!" I still wonder if this is enough to keep all the kids going for two hours, but we'll just have to wing it. "Thanks so much, Craig."

"It's no bother. And as my first ever customer, Alice, I'd like to offer you a discount."

"Really?"

"Yes. And I'd be very grateful if you would let me put out some flyers, and if you'd write me a review as well. If you're happy, of course."

"Craig, mate," says Sam, "you are saving me from having to spend two hours organising Pass the Parcel, and Duck, Duck, Goose. We will be more than happy to write you a review."

"Fantastic! I'd better go and load up, then."

Craig promptly returns to his car and back to town.

"I hope he comes back," I say.

After the initial stress and panic, the party goes brilliantly. I'd thought maybe two hours would be enough, but everyone's having such a good time, and it's such a beautiful evening, many people stay on way longer. At about half-six, Mum and Dad arrive, bringing Karen and Ron with them. Ben is too busy to really pay much attention to his grandparents, and they happily sidle over to the Mowhay for a drink and some food. The bouncy castles are a huge success, and Craig stays close by the outdoor one, supervising and making sure the kids take it in turns. He has them all laughing, and I already know what I want to write in his review. He has brought a ball pit with him as well as the little indoor bouncy castle, and I realise I had no need to worry about whether we would have trouble keeping the kids entertained.

Julie has prepared trays of sandwiches, vol-au-vents, bruschetta and vegetarian scotch eggs, with potato wedges, breadsticks, vegetable sticks and dips. There are jugs of home-made lemonade, water with cucumber and mint, and Fruit Shoots for the kids. Then there is the cake. My mum has made this, and she's outdone herself. It is a chocolate cake in the shape of Duggee from *Hey Duggee*. The kids love it, and there are a few tears when they discover they are not allowed any right now – but the promise of a piece to take home, combined with the arrival of the brownies and flapjacks that Julie has baked soon has them smiling again.

Lizzie comes over to wish Ben a happy birthday, and accepts our invitation to stay and celebrate (and eat) with us. She ends up organising an impromptu yoga session for some of the kids, who just find it all so easy, bending and stretching and crouching with ease.

By around eight, the majority of the guests have gone, leaving the four of us, and Luke, Julie and Zinnia, Mum, Dad, Karen, Ron, Lizzie, and Craig. There is a lot of cleaning up to do, and there are a lot of presents to open.

"Shall we save some for tomorrow?" I suggest to Sam.

"Good idea."

While Julie, Sam, Luke and I tidy things up, Ben has his presents from his grandparents, and a few from his friends, then we surreptitiously move the rest to the boot of the car. Our birthday boy is beyond tired now, and I'm glad that tomorrow he and Holly will be with Karen. They can chill out and nap when they need to.

But before we go our separate ways, I bring out two bottles of prosecco that I've had tucked away in the fridge. There is enough for a glass for each of the adults, to toast Ben, and each other. I'm glad that Craig stays for one, and have noticed that Dad is chatting away to him. I had a feeling they'd get on.

Before he goes, Craig thanks me again. "I won't forget this, Alice – you gave me my first job down here."

"Honestly, Craig, you saved the day!" I smile. "I'll be writing that review tomorrow. And I think lots of people took your cards and flyers. Hopefully things will start to take off over summer."

"If I stay," he says.

"If?"

"Yes, I'm not sure I did the right thing, coming here. It was impetuous, really. Typical of me." His big, friendly face looks downcast.

"That's the only way to do it, Craig! If we thought too hard about everything, nothing would happen! Honestly, Julie talked me into coming down here. If she hadn't, I'd still be at World of Stationery."

"You worked there?" His eyes light up. "With Jason?"

"Yes… Jason Wilberforce. Do you know him?"

"He's my cousin."

"Isn't it a small world?" I smile. "Well, say hello to him from me. And I hope you do decide to stay. Give it a go, at least. You've had a ridiculously rough start, you must still be shaken from the weekend."

"Yes, well, another stupid thing I've done."

"You were unlucky, that's all. Loads of people take risks by the sea, and get away with it. I think until you've lived here a while, it's hard to understand just how powerful and dangerous it can be." Do I sound patronising? I hope not.

"Yes, well, I know now," he says seriously. Then he puts a smile on his face. "Well, we'll see, anyway. I'm renting my place for a year, so I guess I should give it that long, at least."

"Definitely! Who knows what might happen in that time?"

"Yes, it's amazing what can happen in a year."

I smile at him. I find I want to hug him, but that would

110

definitely be inappropriate. It's just there is an air of sadness about Craig, which I hadn't noticed before. I walk with him to his van, and I stand in the car park while he drives off, waving to him before he disappears between the trees.

Then I return to my family and friends, and find Lizzie has got a fire going, and Julie is making coffee and hot chocolate. Holly falls asleep in my arms, while Ben seems to be enjoying a second wind, and he and Zinnia play around the tables. We stay until dusk creeps in, chatting and watching the sparks from the fire flicker into the air. Then we lock up and say our goodbyes to Lizzie, and each other, and form a little convoy of cars, headlights cutting through the twilight as we drive towards the town.

15

It's hot in the club and the bassline of the music shudders through the floorboards as I sway almost imperceptibly in time with the beat. It reminds me of a dream I had, more years ago than I care to remember, where I'd thought those hands belonged to Sam, but they had in fact been those of my old boss Jason Wilberforce, who I still can't believe is Craig's cousin. I remember waking up, and realising I was back in the little room at the top of David's house. I might not have had Sam with me, but at least there was no Jason either – and best of all, I was back in the town I'd fallen in love with a decade before.

It must be nearly as long since I've been in a club like this, and there's a good reason for that. More than one good reason, in fact. I'm not eighteen. I'm not even twenty-eight. But Karen is older still, and that is certainly not stopping her. I envy my own mum, who had a ready-made excuse to escape this hen do. "The Sail Loft," she said. "Phil will need me. Our guests will need me. It's high season now, I can't afford to be away for a night. I'm sorry, Karen. Maybe we can catch up for a meal one night before the big day."

"That's quite alright, Sue," Karen had said sweetly, and I suspect she was thinking that this kind of thing would be way off the mark for Mum anyway. She wouldn't be wrong.

Julie, too, has managed to escape. "I'm so sorry," she said, "but I've got the catering to do at Amethi. There's nobody available to fill in."

Karen had looked disappointed. She had no doubt earmarked Julie as a bit of a wild one, which was certainly true in the past, but Julie's really changed these last few years. "What if Jon comes over with Janie?" Karen asked. "He could do it, couldn't he? He used to work there, it can't be that hard."

I saw Julie swallow. She never appreciates people underestimating quite how difficult her job is.

"I don't think Jonathan can leave his own job to help us out," I had said, quickly stepping in. "He's already taking time off for the wedding, isn't he?"

It's a marvel that Janie is coming, to be honest, but I think she had caved in to Karen's emotional blackmail. And, as she works from home and can work essentially anywhere in the world, she couldn't really come up with a good excuse to stay in Spain.

"But covid…" she'd said when the subject was first broached. Karen had her on speakerphone when we were out in the garden one afternoon. I idly imagined Janie's words floating up into the air, being carried across the rooftops, and out to sea.

"It's on its way out," said her mum. "And besides, they're allowing travel to and from Spain, so we've got to go with what they're saying, haven't we? Follow the science."

You weren't saying that about face masks, or even the vaccine, I thought, but diplomatically kept my opinions to myself.

"OK, Mum," I could hear the resignation in Janie's voice. But she picked it up a notch. "OK, it sounds like fun." I had smiled. At least I had one comrade.

"Sophie's coming too," Karen said.

"Is she?" both Janie and I registered our surprise.

"Yes! Need some young blood, don't we? No offence, you two."

"None taken."

Sam had his back to us, helping Holly up the little plastic slide, but I could sense the smirk on his face.

"So that's six of us, then," I said. We had Karen, and her friends Prue and Meredith (or Poo and Merry as Karen calls them), then me, Janie and Sophie. "Unless Kate's coming too?" I asked hopefully.

"No, she's got to work, hasn't she? Oh, she does work hard."

So far, there is no sign of Sophie. She's meeting us here, she says, and has some accommodation already sorted out as some of her mates from Devon are also down here this weekend. Personally, I suspect she's not going to turn up. She's eighteen, and in Newquay. She's not going to want to hang out with her grandma, grandma's mates, auntie and stepmum. Thank god for Janie, I think.

Karen, Poo and Merry are all on the dancefloor, and I've got to hand it to them, they've certainly got a lot of energy. I feel for the young blokes dancing nearby, though. No doubt on the lookout to pull, they hadn't bargained on being accosted by three sixty-somethings determined to have the night of their lives.

"She's getting married," I can just about hear Merry screeching to one of the blokes. He's definitely young enough to be her grandson. "Give her a snog, she's not going to be available for long." She and Prue cackle loudly, and Karen gives Merry a shove, but she's looking intently at the poor guy, as though sizing him up. I want to get in there and rescue him. *I* feel maternal towards him, for god's sake! He is definitely too young for Karen.

Janie returns with our drinks, bumping gently against my arm. "Here you go, Alice."

"Thanks, Janie." I clink my bottle against hers. It's a semi-warm cider, but it will do. I don't want to drink too much. I quite want to get back to the hotel. I am really hoping that in the morning I can have a quiet swim in the pool, maybe even lie on one of the loungers and have a read, while Karen and her friends sleep off their hangovers.

"Have you seen your mum?" I ask.

"I can't look. Honestly."

"Well, she's having a good time."

"She does seem happy, doesn't she?"

"Yes! And how about you, Janie? And Jon?" It's very hard to gauge how things are over the phone, or our occasional video calls. They've had a tough time of it over the last couple of years, and it looked for a while like they might be about to split up.

"We're good thanks, Alice," Janie smiles, and I think she is telling the truth. Perhaps the move to Spain was the best thing they could have done.

"Has Jonathan been OK?"

I don't want to open up old wounds, but I am well aware of the precarious nature of Jon's mental health. You would never know, when you first meet him. He is to all the world confident and sure of himself. He's very good looking, and charming, and a talented chef, but I know better than to think this means his life is charmed.

115

"He has," Janie leans towards me so I can hear better. "He's been on some tablets, for quite a while, and he's having counselling too, from an ex-pat. He might be getting better at Spanish, but I don't think he's up to explaining his deepest, darkest feelings just yet!"

"Well, that sounds very positive. I'm really glad. And have you two got any plans…"

Oh my god. Am I about to ask if they're planning to get married? To have kids? What am I turning into? Luckily, Janie doesn't take it like this, or at least she chooses not to.

"Yes, we've both got some time off in September, and we're going to Portugal for a couple of weeks. I can't wait."

"Well that sounds lovely." Two weeks in Portugal. Child-free. I can see the appeal of these being the only kind of plans on someone's mind.

"Alice! Janie!" I am taken by surprise by a hug from behind, and I manage to slosh cider all over myself.

"Oh, sorry, Alice," Sophie giggles.

"It wouldn't be the first time, would it?" I smile, delighted to see her. "I didn't really think you'd come."

"Of course I've come. It's Granny's hen do. I've never been to a hen do before."

"Really?" I ask, but of course she hasn't… she's only eighteen. "This will be the first of many, I'm sure. But you may never have another one quite like this."

Karen, Poo and Merry have their handbags on the floor and are strutting their stuff to Tina Turner. As Sophie hugs Janie, I scan the faces of the onlookers. There are smirks and semi-hidden laughter but, if I'm not mistaken, there is also a little bit of admiration. Fair play to Sam's mum and her mates. Why shouldn't they be out there enjoying themselves like this? And there goes Sophie, dancing up to them. My god, she's tall and beautiful and willowy, taking after her beautiful mum. I watch my mother-in-law and my stepdaughter jump up and down, hugging each other, and I scan the same faces again. Some of the young men are looking quite differently on the scene now. Sophie dances good-naturedly and then, as the song ends and she goes to move back to us, an approach is made. I watch with interest. It's hard to tell how old this bloke is, but I'd say early twenties. He's confident – presumptuous, even – walking towards Sophie with a drink. He smiles, and holds it out to her. She returns his smile, accepts the drink, and then snakes an arm around his neck and kisses him.

I am gobsmacked. Karen is less so. She, and her cackling friends, holler approval, while Janie and I look at each other, lost for words.

16

"That is so inappropriate!" I say, though I am smiling.

"You were young once, Alice!" Janie teases. "I bet you were just as bad at Sophie's age!"

"I don't mean Sophie, I mean your mum and her mates!"

We watch with interest as Sophie takes the young man's hand and speaks to Karen and her friends. I had been slightly taken aback initially but watching them, it appears that the two are not strangers who have just met. There is a familiarity in their body language. Karen points in our direction, and waves us over. I really don't want to enter the fray on the dancefloor, but as Sophie and her… friend… are both looking at us, I don't think there is much choice.

"Come on," I say to Janie, "let's find out what's going on."

Unfortunately, the DJ puts *Place Your Hands On* by Glastonbury band Reef just as we step down, and a load more people barrel onto the dancefloor, jumping about and shouting the anthem as loud as they can. It makes first introductions quite awkward.

"This is…" I can't make out his name, but he is smiling at me and holding out his hand. I shake it as best I can, and try to gauge how old he is. Sophie looks older than her eighteen years, but this guy looks older still. And he hasn't got the excuse of heavy make-up to add to this effect.

"Sorry, who?" I say to Sophie, who is closer to my ear.

"Rory," I think she says.

"Hi," I smile at him, and "Rory," I say to Janie, right next to me.

"And how old is Rory?" she says into my ear; at least I think that's what she says. I'm glad she's thinking along the same lines as me. I don't think I can ask him that, though.

"Sophie, I'm too old for this!" I say, hugging her. "I'm going back to the bar. Come and find us in a bit."

"I will," she hugs me exuberantly. I can see how happy she is. That's the important thing. But will Sam see it that way?

The rest of the weekend passes slightly more sedately. I think Karen had got what she wanted from that first night, and the following day she is happy to lounge around in the hotel. Her friends, however, have abandoned us for another 'sesh' and night out. Karen didn't seem to mind.

"They're single, aren't they? Looking for love." We are on the loungers by the hotel pool, drying off after a swim.

"I don't know if they're going to find it in Newquay," I say.

"When did you become so cynical, Alice?" Karen smiles at me. "I bet people said you and Sam wouldn't last. Just a holiday romance."

"True," I grudgingly admit.

"And you and Jonathan," Karen says to Janie, who is reclining on the lounger on Karen's other side. "That was a bolt from the blue, wasn't it? Who knows what life might offer up, as long as we're open to it."

"You sound like Lizzie!" I say. "But you're right. Maybe I'll eat my words."

"They're nice women," she says. "They might be a bit rough round the edges, but they've both got hearts of gold. They're just a bit lonely, too."

"I can see that. And I know they're important to you. Friends like that are irreplaceable."

"I missed them, when I was in Spain."

"I can imagine."

"I missed Sam, too, even though he'll never believe that."

"Well, you know…" I feel a bit awkward now. Obviously, I know how Sam feels about it, but it's not my place to tell her.

"It was a selfish decision, to go. Tough on you too, Janie." She turns to her daughter, who shrugs.

"Life's too short for regrets, Mum," she says. "And if you hadn't gone to Spain, who knows how life might have gone? Maybe it would have been better. Maybe it would have been much worse. We can't possibly know. But Sam and I have turned out alright, haven't we?"

"More than alright," Karen sniffles. I suspect she is weakened somewhat by her hangover. Maybe she's still even a bit drunk. "I'm so proud of you both. And you, Alice, and your beautiful children. Sophie, too. I don't deserve you all."

"Don't talk daft, Karen," I lay a hand on her arm. "We are very lucky to have you, too. I hope you know that. And I'm not just saying that to make you feel better. I mean it."

She sniffs again, and I realise she's not the only one with a tear in her eye. My god, I'm more emotional than ever these days.

"Talking of Sophie…" I say, needing to move the conversation on.

"And her young man!" Karen says.

"Or not so young…" Janie grins.

"How old do you think he is?" I ask.

"He's got to be mid-twenties, at least. When Sophie comes here later, I'll ask her. Unless he's with her, of course."

"She said she'd be coming alone. She's going to have dinner with us then head back out to find her friends."

"*Friends*," Karen sniggers. "Oh, to be that young again."

And we all go quiet; I think each of us is contemplating how life has changed since we were Sophie's age. Sometimes for the better, sometimes for the worse. But we've all had our time of being eighteen, and one day Sophie will be looking back at hers, too. I hope that she makes the most of right now, and enjoys this time as much as she can, before responsibilities start to seep in and place limits on her freedom. Having said that, I don't fancy being the one to tell Sam about Sophie's new boyfriend.

"Grandma!" Sophie exclaims, walking into the hotel dining room fifteen minutes late but brimming with smiles and a confidence that can only be admired.

"Don't call me that, it makes me feel old!" Karen admonishes, standing and hugging Sophie.

I do the same, as does Janie, then we sit, settling ourselves, and I'm struck by the fact that this is the first time we've ever been alone, just the four of us like this.

"Look at all of us Branvall women!" I say. "Well – Collins in your case, Sophie, but you know what I mean. We should have Holly here, as well." I feel like my heart does an extra little beat as I think of my girl, tucked up in her bed at home. It's so funny to be just sitting down to eat at seven; which normally means children's bedtimes, and then hopefully an hour or two relaxing before Sam and I cave in and head off to bed, too. Seven has come to mark the day winding to a close. Now, our night is just beginning. Having said that, I'd say we three older ones would happily be in bed in a couple of hours. Sophie, of course, looks as fresh as a daisy.

"We've been trying not to envy you, Soph," I say, smiling and squeezing her hand. "Your youth…"

"Your boyfriend!" Janie adds cheekily.

Sophie blushes.

"So how did you meet Rory?" I ask.

"Out clubbing, in Exeter," she says airily.

"Is that where he lives?" I want to know more about him, but I don't want it to sound like an inquisition.

"Yes, well he's at uni there."

I let out a little inward sigh of relief. If he's at uni, he won't be that much older than her. A respectable two or three years, at most. "Oh, that's good. What's he studying?"

At this point, the waiter comes to take our orders. We order some wine to go with the meal, and four glasses. It feels funny, having Sophie sitting at a table with us as an equal. But I like it, too. I'm also relieved that the interruption has broken my conveyor belt of questions. Sophie turns to Karen and asks her about the wedding plans.

"Well, you know, we're a bit limited, due to the bloody stupid restrictions, but it's going to be just perfect," Karen says. "We've booked the church for the ceremony and then the reception at the Beach Bar, courtesy of Sam's friend Andrew. Christian's providing the catering – you know, from the Cross-Section – and Ron's mates' band will be playing, and we're hoping for a nice long evening with a beautiful sunset, and dancing on the beach into the small hours. If we'd had it a week later, then we'd be able to have far more people. To be honest, it's quite nice limiting the numbers because we've had to really think about who we want to be there."

"Tricky too, though, I bet," says Janie. "You don't want to offend anyone."

"No, it's alright, really. We just tell people we'd love to have invited them – even if there's not a chance in hell we would have done!" She cackles, and I can't help but laugh.

Karen lists the guests. I'm quite pleased it will be such a small wedding, with thirty people including her and Ron. For one thing, I don't think I am ready for a huge social event. I am sure that over time these things will return to normal, but right now it feels strange, to imagine being in a packed-out church, for example, where pews are squeezed in tightly together and there's not much room for manoeuvre. Will we all come out of this pandemic lacking social skills and suffering from claustrophobia – or even agoraphobia? I really hope not. With a bit of luck these newly-learned considerations, of keeping a distance, and avoiding physical contact, will leave us as quickly as they arrived.

The waiter brings our food, and we all tuck in, a comfortable lull in conversation descending. I am ravenous, I realise, and delighted to be able to eat uninterrupted and without having to help somebody else cut their food up, or use their cutlery, or to have to pick up Holly's water cup that she drops roughly 100,000 times in the course of a meal.

"Could I bring a plus-one, Grandma?" Sophie asks quietly, and it takes me a minute to register what she's said.

She is blushing again.

"Oh, my love, I don't think you can," Karen says. "Do you mean Rory?"

Sophie nods.

"I wish I could say yes, you know I do, but we've already exhausted our quota. Sorry." Karen lays her hand on her granddaughter's.

"That's OK." Sophie looks disappointed, though.

I want to look at Janie, and see if she's thinking what I am. This must be serious.

"Tell you what, if anyone cancels, you're first on the list, OK, sweetie?"

"OK. Thank you."

We move on, to talk of Karen's honeymoon, which she and Ron are delaying until the winter. And life in Spain. "Can I come and visit?" Sophie asks, "Next year, maybe?"

"Of course!" Janie says. "As long as it's OK with your mum and dad." She looks slightly uncomfortable saying this and I know why. Suddenly, Sophie doesn't really seem like the kind of person who needs permission from her parents. But at the same time, we all know she would need some financial help for a trip to Spain. She does have a job, at a supermarket not far from her Devon home, but I suspect that her wages go out almost as quickly as they've come in.

Sophie looks satisfied with this answer, though. I watch her as she finishes her meal, wiping up the pasta sauce with her garlic bread. I am overcome by a wave of raw emotion, which I have to hide. Multiple Sophies run through my mind. The nine-year-old who tipped her bucket of water on me; the ten-year-old who ran off and hid in Luke's dad's shed one terrifying night; the thirteen-year-old who decided she wanted to live with me and Sam, and the fourteen-year-old who realised she actually needed to be with her mum. In just nine years, I've seen her turn from a child into a young adult, and I feel incredibly proud of her.

It's an emotional day, and the red wine is only adding to that. When the waiter comes to clear away our plates, Sophie asks him to bring another bottle. Karen doesn't bat an eyelid, but Janie and I exchange a glance. But Karen has already told her to order whatever she wants: "After all, it's not often I get to treat you all, and I won't be having another hen do!"

And it's nice, I have to say, to sit back and enjoy another glass of wine, and watch Sophie devour a huge Eton Mess, the rest of us all too full to manage another bite. When the waiter asks if we'd like coffee, Janie and I say yes, and Karen says she'll have a whisky, but it seems this is Sophie's cue to leave. She checks her phone. "Rory's outside."

"He's been waiting for you all this time?" I notice Janie is slurring her words a little.

"No, silly, he's driven up!"

"He hasn't been drinking, has he?" I ask before I've thought about how that sounds.

"No, of course not! He's very responsible," Sophie giggles. "He is twenty-five, after all."

"Twenty-five?" I splutter. I can't help myself. "I thought you said he was at uni?"

"He is! He quit the first time round. And the second!" She giggles again. "But he says he's committed now."

Does he, indeed? I am thinking, but I just smile and nod, and give her a hug before she goes. Sam is not going to be happy about this.

17

"Has Sophie mentioned a Rory to you?" I ask Sam, pretend-nonchalantly, as we settle on the sofa on Sunday night. I am shattered after two late nights, and a whole lot more alcohol than I'm used to.

It was lovely to get home, and be greeted with such enthusiasm, by Holly, Ben and Meg – and Sam, whose "Alice!" also suggested a slight feeling of relief. Once I'd been back for a bit, he took himself off for a bike ride, and came back looking hot and sweaty, but somehow refreshed.

"Rory… no, I don't think so. Who is he? A friend from school?"

"Not exactly."

"Boyfriend?" Sam looks amused. I can soon wipe that expression from his face.

"Yes, well, kind of."

"What do you mean, kind of?"

"Well, I don't know if you'd call him a boy, exactly." Even I don't know why I've taken this slightly infuriating tack to introduce him to the prospect of Sophie's new … partner? I quickly pull in the reins. "Well, he's a bit older than her. Seven years older, to be precise."

A quick calculation. "He's twenty-five?"

"Yes," I say, an apology in my voice, though it's hardly my fault.

"But that's… he's an adult."

"He's at uni," I offer, as if that somehow makes him younger.

"So he's twenty-five and still a student? Not even working?" I can feel Sam's righteous indignation begin to fizz and crackle, ignited by his understandable wish to protect Sophie. I know it is even harder for him, being remote for her, and he's struggled these last few years, not feeling like he's been a good enough support for her. Lockdowns were incredibly hard as well, and I know that was the worst part for him, not being able to see his oldest child. She's grown up even more during the time they've been apart. "Does Kate know?"

"I have no idea."

"I'll soon find out." And he's sitting up, phone in hand and elbows on knees, those beautiful shoulders of his now hunched and bunched up with tension. I stay where I am, ruffling Meg's fur and smoothing her ears. "Kate?" I can just hear her cheery greeting. "What's this about Sophie's boyfriend?" I think there is a moment's silence, but then I hear her say something, but I can't make out the words. "So it's true, then?" Sam asks. "Why am I only hearing this now?"

I decide it's better if I make myself scarce, so I go through to the kitchen, Meg wisely following at my heels. I try not to listen to Sam, and instead I put on the radio and the kettle, and busy myself drying up the plates and cutlery from the draining board.

After a while, Sam comes through, and his face looks somehow pinched, as it does when he's stressed. "Twenty-five," he says. "What do you think about that?"

"I think…" I choose my words carefully, knowing it is not

just Sam but Sophie I have to respect here. "I think it's a big age gap, for sure. And I know it will bother you. It bothers me, to be honest. But perhaps it's better to let it run its course. Try to accept it?"

"I just don't know if I can do that, Alice. He's a man. And she's barely an adult. Is she, really? Come on."

"No. I know, she's young. And a seven-year age gap seems huge at her age. But she's quite grown-up, Sam. And he's maybe less so. They probably meet somewhere in the middle."

"I don't think that's making me feel any better, thinking he's immature."

"I didn't say that, exactly."

"But it's implied, isn't it? I mean, he's mid-twenties and going out with an eighteen-year-old. What does that say about him?"

It is a weird, grey area. If he were older, even pushing thirty, it would feel very much wrong to me. Any older than that, I have no doubt that it would have to be stopped – although quite how, I have no idea. But somehow, seven years doesn't seem completely outrageous. I think it is just that she is only eighteen. And she's about to embark on her uni days herself, if her A-level results are as good as expected. So aside from anything else, she doesn't really need a distraction, of any sort, but especially not one in the shape of a half-man, half-child eternal student – no matter how good-looking he might be.

"I think you have to tread carefully, Sam. If you put your foot down, or possibly even if you just hint at disapproval, you might push her away. What did Kate say?"

"Something very similar to that," he admits. "And I know

you're right, both of you. But why the fuck didn't Kate tell me first?"

"Perhaps because she thought you'd react badly?" I venture a small smile.

"Ha! Yeah, well, she'd be right."

"What did she actually say?"

"That she was going to tell me at Mum's wedding, if the thing hadn't already run its course. She says she's met him and he's a nice kid. If 'kid' is the right word. A bit full of himself, she says, very into politics, and the environment, and changing the world."

"You say all that like it's a bad thing."

"Ah, well, I don't mean to. You know you just get a bit more cynical with age."

"Well, that's true." I don't like to point out that this doesn't seem to be a problem for Rory.

"I just don't want her getting her head turned by someone who's not worthy of her. I know what she's like. If he's full of all that shit, she'll be impressed by him. She wants to change the world as well, doesn't she?"

"She does." I did, too, at her age. Where did that go? Swallowed up by the world changing around me. Geoff's controlling ways, and then a need for stability and a regular job. Paying a mortgage. Then a whirlwind return to Cornwall, and my all-consuming relationship with Sam, and starting a business. Becoming a mum. Somewhere along the way, I've lost some of my enthusiasm and drive for making the world a better place.

"I don't know what to say, Sam. I'm sorry. I know it must be really weird. I only met him briefly, but he seemed like a nice bloke. And he was very responsible, picking her up from the hotel after she'd come to dinner with us."

"He hadn't been drinking, had he?"

"That's just what I said! But no, Sophie said he wouldn't."

"Well, that's something, I suppose."

"It is. And look, she's young. And she'll be off on her travels in a few months, and then it will be uni. Her life will change again. She's eighteen. Chances are, she'll meet somebody new, and Rory will be a thing of the past."

"We were eighteen," says Sam.

"Yes, we were." And I don't know how to answer that. Because we were eighteen when we met, and fell in love, and look at us now. It's a bit of a circular argument because our feelings were very much real. And now we are married, with kids, and a mortgage, and I can't bear the thought of life without him. But I don't think he will want to imagine such a future for Sophie and Rory.

18

In David's absence, I tell Martin all the goings-on, and find him just as good a listener as his husband. He and the kids are just out of quarantine after travelling home, and installed in their beautiful house just a little way along the estuary. It's good to be back there, and even though they let the house to another family in their absence, it still feels very much like their home, and the kids clearly feel that way. They entertain Ben and Holly, both of my children in awe of these worldly-wise, older children who have been to Disney World Florida during their time in the States. It gives Martin and me the chance to sit and chat, and he smiles when I describe the situation with Sophie.

"We've got all that to come, I guess," he says. "And I know what I was like at that age. I didn't know if it was boys or girls I liked."

"Really?"

"Yes, well, I mean, I knew really, but I always got on well with girls. And sometimes my feelings became a bit confused, or maybe I just tried to convince myself that what I was feeling was more than just friendship. It was the more acceptable route to take, and seemed like it might have been easier. It would never have worked, though."

"It must have been tough."

"Well… yeah, it was. But it was fun, too!"

I laugh. "And did you have any older partners?"

"No, but when I was in my twenties, I did have a younger boyfriend. God, I was such a Rory!"

That does make me laugh. And the way that Martin has reacted, or failed to react, makes me feel a bit more at ease with the situation. I just want Sam to be the same.

"How's David getting on without you?" I ask.

"He'll be having the time of his life! Young, free and childless, for a few weeks at least. But really, he's finding it tough. Bea's in a state. She's exhausted from covid herself, and she can't sleep for worry about Bob, which means David can't sleep, either."

"And now you're back here, it must be tough for you, too."

"It's a nightmare, to be honest. And those two weeks of quarantine were something I wouldn't do again in a hurry. I mean, now I look back, it doesn't feel like long at all, but I can tell you, getting back here, with two little kids, all of us with jet lag, and missing David, it seemed like a very, very long time."

"Bet your mum and dad are pleased you're back."

"They are." He smiles. "And that is one huge bonus. It was awful being so far away when the news was full of the misery of isolation, not to mention the number of people getting ill and dying. I kept wondering what I'd do if they got it, and if they ended up in hospital... god, all those stories of people saying their goodbyes on FaceTime. It doesn't bear thinking about."

"It feels incredibly unreal, doesn't it?"

"It really does."

"Is there any news on Bob?"

"No. Not yet. I'm worried, Alice, I have to be honest.

Surely there would have been some improvement by now?"

"I don't know. I think it affects everyone differently. I mean, of course you're worried. It would be impossible not to be. But I don't think it necessarily means we should expect the worst."

"That's what I keep telling David."

"I guess it's all we can do, until we know any more."

I message Bea when I'm back home, and send her my love. Then I message David, too. They both reply almost immediately.

From Bea: **It's lovely to hear from you, Alice, and to know you're thinking about me. About us. I miss him all the time, but I just have to hope he's coming back to me. Bxxx**

And from David: **Thanks, Alice. I'm glad you've seen M, T & E today. I miss them so much it hurts. But I can't leave Bea right now. I just hope we get some good news soon. And I want to come home. More than ever.** There is a pause and I begin a reply to him but another message bumps in: **Especially now Sophie's got an older man. Can't wait to meet him ;-)**

Like I'd let you near him, I reply. **He's much too good-looking, and young.**

I do feel like I'm missing out on all the fun. When's Karen's wedding?

Not long now! But she's got to keep it low-key anyway, with the restrictions on numbers.

Are you saying I'm not important enough to warrant an invite?

That is exactly what I'm saying. You'd be something like 386ᵗʰ on the list.

Fine.

I can imagine David smiling as we have this exchange, and I am glad to be able to be light-hearted with him. It must be incredibly hard for him and Bea at the moment. I can't imagine being able to tease her in the same way; not just because it's her husband who's ill, but I don't have quite the same kind of relationship with her that I do with her brother. I just hope that Bob recovers, and that David is able to return to us soon.

19

Saturday July 31st is the day of Karen and Ron's wedding. I take Meg out for an early walk along the beach. No dogs are allowed later in the day at this time of year, and rightly so, really. Anyway, it's much better for us both to be out at this hour, before the beach is gradually coloured in by deckchairs, windbreaks and beach tents.

We are not the only walkers out, of course, and we see some familiar faces. Meg definitely has her favourite dogs, who she will go zipping around with, chasing back and forth, and very often barrelling straight into my legs. I love seeing her like this, and I feel like I'd love to chase around with them, too, although in reality of course I'd be out of breath within a minute. We humans are not really built for the contours of the beach, either. The undulating surface and occasional human-built hole which Meg navigates with ease hold considerable potential for twisted ankles, not to mention embarrassment.

It's a blowy day today, and the sand is determined to get in my eyes and my hair. I hope that the wind dies down in time for the wedding reception, although I can see that the early-bird surfers appreciate it.

I walk the full length of the beach, taking a few moments at the far end to stop and rest against the rocks, Meg lying panting at my feet, also glad of the rest. I stop to ruffle the fur on her head, and then sit next to her, not minding the damp seeping through my clothes. I gaze out across the expanse of the beach, and skim my vision across the waves. No dolphins today, or at least none that I can see. I know I only have a finite amount of time to rest here, but I will make the most of it, for today promises to be a hectic day.

Back at home, Sam and the kids have had their breakfast, and Sam is rushing about, clearing up, unable to relax, and therefore finding things to do.

"Meg!" he groans as she trots through, leaving a trail of sandy, wet footprints in her wake.

"Sorry!" I say. "We had a proper paddle, but I thought she'd have dried off by now."

"You don't look much cleaner yourself," he smiles, taking in the sight of my damp, sandy clothes.

"I thought I'd wear this to the wedding," I say. "No good?"

"Who am I to tell you what to wear?"

"Great. It's settled then!" I reach up and kiss him. "Feeling nervous?"

"Is it obvious?"

"Only to me."

"You'd think it was me that's getting married! But you know what I'm like with speeches…"

"And emotions!"

"Hey! I'm not that bad!"

"At least it's only a small gathering," I say. "You don't have to speak in front of a huge crowd of people."

"I don't know if that's worse, in a way."

"I know what you mean. But you'll be great. You know you will."

I go through to the kitchen to sort out Meg's breakfast and put the kettle on, then I head upstairs for a shower. It takes a couple of washes to rid my scalp of the grainy feeling, and that will all be in vain if it's still windy out there later. But I'd better look my best for my mother-in-law's wedding.

It's a lovely thing, to get married later in life (don't tell Karen I said that), and I think it says a lot about hope and positivity, and of course love. I am so lucky to have parents who have stayed together, and who still love each other and for the most part get on so well. They're even surviving running a business together, which is no small matter. When I was younger, it felt like all families were like mine. I sometimes felt sorry for myself that I didn't have a sibling, but I didn't realise how lucky I was, with such a safe and stable home. It was really only once I reached secondary school that I began to see how very different life is for some people. I met Julie, and she was the first friend I had whose dad was not around. Which seems crazy now, when I come to think of it, but I suppose it reflects the area and the time that I grew up in.

I step out of the shower and dry off in the bathroom, then I open the expensive moisturiser that Sophie got me for my birthday. It smells lovely, and I take my time massaging it in. I am normally a dry-off-throw-some clothes-on kind of person, but today feels special.

"You smell nice," Sam says when I walk through to the bedroom. He is nervously pacing.

"Thanks!" I say, and I laugh, "Calm down, would you? You're making me nervous!"

"I'm going to have a shower myself, then I'll go on down to Mum's, if you don't mind?"

"Of course I don't! Will Sophie be there already?"

"She should be. And Janie."

"And Mum will be down about lunchtime." I feel a little left out, but there really would not be room for me, Ben and Holly as well, and I don't think a four-year-old and a toddler are conducive to preparing for a wedding anyway. Dad is coming here after he's dropped Mum off at Karen's, so we can make our way to the wedding together. Ron stayed at his brother's last night, so he and Karen won't see each other until she gets to the church. I love the romance of it.

I go downstairs and find that I seem to have caught Sam's nerves, and I fuss around, wanting time to just fly by. I think perhaps that having not been able to do very much socially for so long makes anything like this seem that little bit more special.

Sam comes downstairs, his suit carrier over his shoulder, and he kisses me then goes to the kitchen table, where Holly and Ben are busy gluing scraps of paper to a larger piece of paper, and also to their fingers, and he kisses them, too. "Be good for Mummy, won't you? See you at Granny's wedding!"

"Bye, Daddy." Holly threatens to glue herself to him too, proffering chubby, sticky fingers, but he manages to dodge them.

"See you at the church!" I call as he leaves. He turns and smiles, then he's on his way.

The gluing all done, we have some lunch, and then I run a bath for Ben and Holly. I coat them both in bubbles so that they laugh and try to throw handfuls at me. I'm glad I haven't got changed yet. And once they are out and both dry, and dressed in their wedding outfits – cute little blue dress for Holly and a polo shirt and shorts for Ben, I look at my watch and realise I have only about fifteen minutes left for myself. How did that happen? I bring them into my room, and they sit on the bed, Holly watching Ben play *Paddington Run* on my tablet, while I wriggle into my dress and brush my hair, applying my make-up in a very hurried fashion.

"Hello?" I hear from downstairs. And then, "Hello Meg! No, no, don't jump up. These are my best togs." Dad has let himself in.

"I'm just getting ready, Dad!" I call. "The kids are up here, too. We'll be down in a bit."

"No rush, love," he calls and, having heard his voice, both my son and daughter are scrambling off the bed, desperate to go and say hello. Which buys me a little bit of time to just give myself a critical once-over. I will have to do. I pull on my cardigan, grab my bag, and leave the room.

At the church, where there might normally be so many wedding-goers milling around, in these sad, diminished times, there is just Ron's brother, Brian, to greet people.

We say hi, and go on in. At the front of the church, Ron is sitting very still, facing straight ahead. Ron's daughter Stella is sitting behind him, with her grown-up son Stan and his family. We sit on the opposite pew to them, leaving a row in front for Mum, Janie and Sophie to sit.

Prue and Meredith arrive, looking like they may have had a drink or two beforehand. They smile and wave as they walk up the aisle, and say hello just a tad too loudly, then shuffle into the pew behind us.

There are just a handful of other people to come, and

even once everyone has arrived, it is only the front five rows on either side of the church that are taken. Jonathan, my old chef, old friend, and Janie's boyfriend, has come in last, narrowly missing being late. I can't wait to see him later.

There are cushions and signs on the seats, asking people to keep a space between themselves and others. It almost takes the edge off proceedings, but not quite. As the organ strikes up, we stand and turn as one, to see Mum, followed by Karen and Sam, followed by Sophie and Janie. I catch my breath at the sight of these people, each so important to me, walking slowly and purposefully up the central aisle. Mum smiles at all of us, and Holly waves madly, then Karen and Sam – Karen's eyes fixed straight ahead, but Sam's flickering across to me – and then Janie and Sophie. Holly can barely contain herself, but Ben stands very solemnly, having been primed about weddings, and determined to be very grown-up in comparison to his baby sister.

As she reaches the front, Mum steps to the side, and Sam and his mum draw parallel to Ron. I see his shoulders are shaking, and I wonder if he's laughing, but as he turns his head to look at his wife-to-be, I see that he is actually crying. My own reactive tears catch me unawares, and I choke back a sob, aware that Ben is watching me closely. I look down and smile at him. He looks back at me, puzzled.

It is a lovely service. Karen and Ron have written their own vows. They're beautiful.

Ron, holding Karen's hands in his, says: "I promise to love you and cherish you, and take care of you, so we can build our lives together, intertwined and together forever."

Karen's are longer: "I love you more than words can say, but I'll have a go anyway." There is a little grateful laughter at this. "Since you've come into my life, Ron, I've been happier than I ever thought it possible to be. You make me a better person, and I promise to stay true and faithful, and love you forever."

I look at Sam, who is sitting in front of me, with Sophie next to him, and Janie then Mum on the other side of her. Sophie also glances at Sam, and they share a smile.

And then almost as soon as it has begun, or so it feels, the wedding ceremony is over. We follow the married couple down the aisle, emerging into the day with that familiar feeling of elation at Ron and Karen's union, tinged with relief that everything has gone as planned. There are a few friends of the newly-married couple, out in the churchyard. They cheer and throw confetti.

I fight my initial thought, which is whether this is strictly in line with covid restrictions. Nothing like a good virus to suck the romance out of a moment.

Nigel, who is a friend of Ron's from way back, is also unofficial wedding photographer, and he seems to be everywhere, snapping shots from behind gravestones, and around the ancient stone walls of the church.

And then Brian, who is not only Ron's brother but also the taxi-driver I have relied on many times over the years, whisks Ron and Karen away, and down to the beach, leaving the rest of us to walk on behind. We make a merry bunch, heading through town, and people stop to look at us, many smiling and wishing the happy couple well.

Sam whisks Ben onto his shoulders, to save his little legs, and I do the same with Holly, glad that I chose relatively sensible shoes. Prue and Meredith had perhaps not thought through the practicalities of a reception on the beach, or even having to traverse the steep streets of the town, and they soon remove their painful-looking heels, happy to walk barefoot. Despite the rush of wind as we round the corner towards the beach, it is far calmer than it was this morning, and it's with great pleasure that we all head down onto the soft sands and towards the Beach Bar, where Karen and Ron await us. As do glasses of champagne, and apple juice for the children.

There is ivory-and-gold bunting, and the chairs are decorated with elegant bows. Brian has made a second trip to the church, to collect the flower arrangements, and he and his wife Sandra are busy setting them up in the corners of the room and along the bar.

The place soon fills up, with our quota of thirty, and it's just busy enough that the room is filled with laughter and talk. I sit Ben and Holly on one of the bean bags by the window, and Sophie comes to sit with us.

"You look beautiful!" I say, kissing her. "Doesn't your sister look nice, you two?"

Ben's not too fussed either way, but Holly enthusiastically throws herself at Sophie, putting her pudgy arms around her neck. Sophie laughs, somehow managing to put her glass on the table without spilling a drop, and cuddling Holly, which turns into a tickle, which has my little girl helpless with laughter.

Jonathan and Janie join us, and I sink back into my seat, absolutely content, and full of love; for the people gathered round me, for life, and for love itself.

We sit and enjoy the view; the beach is busy, and packed with holiday-makers. It feels very exclusive to have this place to ourselves. And as the afternoon flies by, with more drinks, and snacks, and a myriad of photos, the sands begin to reveal themselves more fully, as deckchairs and windbreaks and beach tents are folded up and packed away, and empty cool bags and tote bags heavy with wet swimming gear are slung over people's arms. The crowds retreat, seeping back into town like seawater into sand, thinking of what they'll have for tea, or restaurant bookings, or a night in the pub, and the beach is all but forgotten.

And slowly, like a snail pushing its head shyly out of its shell, we come out of the bar, bringing chairs and tables and bean bags, and we stake our claim on a little bit of this beautiful place, which can be ours just for tonight.

Andrew has done fish fingers and chips for Ben and Holly, and he and Becky have said they will take them home to stay at theirs for the night. So I sit with my children while they eat their tea, and they stay longer and later than they might normally do, and then Becky appears, her own child Zach holding onto her hand. He is very welcome in Ben's eyes, and the two of them hatch a plan to build an enormous sandcastle, only to be thwarted by Becky telling them it is time to go home. Still, Ben is excited at the thought of a sleepover, so he doesn't take too much persuading, and Holly – though reluctant at first to leave me – does not put up too much of a fight, and I see her lay her head on Becky's shoulder as they move away.

Luke is looking after Meg this evening, and Lizzie and Julie are managing everything at Amethi, so I am now free to let my hair down, and enjoy myself.

20

Poor old Sam is not quite off the hook yet. There is still the meal, and the requisite speeches, to go.

Thankfully, Christian's a little behind schedule, with two of his staff calling in with covid (what else?), so it is decided to bring the speeches forward while we await our dinner.

Sam is up first. "It's a blessing, really," I tell him.

"Easy for you to say," he grumbles.

"Yep!" I grin. I'm on my fourth glass of champagne, I'm child-free, and enjoying life.

"Wish me luck," he says, and he's off. He gets a spoon and tings his glass, and it doesn't take long for this small gathering to go quiet.

"Hello everyone," Sam says, and clears his throat. I know it's a sign of nerves with him, and I feel my stomach contract a little, on his behalf. I try to catch his eye, so as to send him an encouraging smile, but he is steadfastly not looking at me. "As you all know, I'm Karen's son, Sam." A little cheer goes up. "And as many of you know, Mum and I have not always had the easiest relationship." I glance at Karen, to see how she reacts to that, but she's just gazing at her son, and I think I even detect a little nod. "But these last few years, things have changed. Mum came back to Cornwall, and maybe I wasn't the most welcoming, to begin with. But it's like… it's like we've…" Oh my god, he's having to stifle some tears. I glance at Karen again, and see her eyes are shining, too. Janie moves next to me and squeezes my hand. I put my arm around her, and give her a little squeeze. Sam clears his throat. Continues. "It's like we've got to know each other all over again. When Mum left, I was sixteen. Just left school. A little full of myself. Determined to be a champion surfer and travel the world, just me and my board." Some laughter here. "When she came back, I was a dad, and my whole life had changed." He does look at me now, and he smiles. I return his smile, almost shyly. "But it wasn't just me that had changed. Mum had, too, and it took me a while to realise that. And then she met Ron, and she changed again. Because I don't think I have ever known her to be so happy. And I've never seen her smile so much. I'm grateful to you both – to Mum, for coming back, and for being here for me and Alice and Sophie, Ben and Holly – and to Ron, for making my mum so bloody happy! I wish you both a long, happy and healthy life together. To Mum... to Karen... and Ron."

Sam raises his glass, the relief evident on his face, to me at least. And I raise my glass, echoing his toast loudly, my voice mingling with so many others. Sam stands for a moment, then gratefully slinks across to us, to listen to Ron, and then Brian. Both make us laugh, both make us cry. I suspect we are all grateful for the release. And then Christian and a couple of his staff arrive, and we all file back inside to take our designated seats.

While we have been out on the beach, Andrew has rearranged the tables to make a more formal arrangement inside. Christian's staff busy themselves unpacking and plating up our meals, which have been individually ordered and prepared, then they bring them to us, at our designated seats, and remove the covers to reveal beautiful, colourful, delicious-smelling food. There are bottles of red and white wine on the tables, and jugs of water brimming with ice, lemon and cucumber.

"I'm starving!" Sam says, wasting no time in tucking into his dinner.

I follow suit. I have a roasted aubergine stuffed with peppers, onion, rice and chilli, accompanied by some delicious warm Turkish pide bread and salads. It is mouth-wateringly delicious, and I clean my plate, feeling like I could eat the same again.

"What do you think, Jon?" I ask our professional chef.

"Not bad…" he grins. "OK, then, it's brilliant." He has had sea bass with sautéed spinach and potatoes, with grilled tomatoes on the side and a small jug of some pale yellow sauce. "I do miss Cornish fish."

"But not too much?" Janie says hopefully.

I feel for the two of them, both coming from different places. It's a bit of a balancing act, making sure they are both happy. And I know I'm not from Cornwall originally, but I didn't move here to be with Sam. I knew that I wanted to be here because I love this place. Sam was just a bonus.

"No. Not too much!" He kisses her, and at the same time Karen bursts onto the scene.

"Your turn next, you two!" she says.

Jonathan blushes and Janie says, "Mum!"

"Just kidding. But I tell you what, I'd recommend it to anyone, this getting married business! What a day!"

I stand and pull a chair over for her to join us. She sits between me and Sam.

"Thank you, son," she says.

"What for?"

"That speech. I won't forget it, ever. And thank you for… for forgiving me."

"Who says I've forgiven you?" Sam asks. But he is smiling, and he puts his arms round his mum, and hugs her. I've never really noticed before, how small she seems next to him, and perhaps I've never really seen Sam hug her quite like this before.

Outside, the light is fading gently, and the beach is close to empty. Later, I will see if I can get Sam to come for a walk with me. We can take off our shoes, and walk barefoot in the moonlit shallows. But for now, I want to stay here, in the heart of this happiness. I pour myself another glass of wine, sit back, and sigh.

21

Unfortunately, the romantic walk is not to be. While the beach sinks into darkness, and the wine takes hold, we wedding-goers mix more, and the band begins to play. There is dancing, and laughing, and… an exclamation. Loud enough for me to hear, from the other side of the room. And loud enough to make most people look around.

I know immediately that it is Sam, and I push my way through, to see him standing with an upset-looking Sophie, and a sheepish-looking Rory.

"What is he doing here, Sophie?" Sam is asking his daughter, and her face turns a vivid shade of red.

"He's my boyfriend, Dad."

"And he's not invited." Sam says firmly. "You know there's a strict guest list."

I know that he's using this as an excuse for not being able to deal with Sophie having an older boyfriend. I glance again at Rory, who actually looks a bit scared. And he looks younger than his twenty-five years, to me.

"But Holly and Ben have gone, Dad," Sophie says petulantly, "so there's space for two more people. And there's only one of Rory."

A good job, too, I think.

"That is not the point, Sophie, and you know it."

By this point, everyone else is trying very hard to act like they don't know anything is going on. It is just me, Sam, Sophie and Rory. I try to make sure I think before I speak. I've had a number of drinks today, and I may not be in the right state to be diplomatic. But here goes…

"Sam, Rory's here now. Hi, Rory," I offer as an aside, and Rory smiles gratefully. "And Soph's right, we are two down, so one extra person…"

Sam looks at me like I'm betraying him. Have I done the wrong thing? Should I be backing him up, unquestioningly?

Sophie latches onto my words. "Exactly, Dad. And Rory's my boyfriend. And this is a family party. I'm eighteen, for god's sake."

"Eighteen!" Sam tuts.

"What, Dad? You were eighteen when you met Alice." I have a feeling this argument is going to be wheeled out time and again. "And look at you now. You've got two kids, you're married…"

"Exactly."

Now my hairs are bristling. What's he saying? That it's so bad, to be married and have kids? *Calm down, Alice*, my inner voice soothes me. *That is not what he's saying at all, and you know it.*

Rory is staring at his feet. I take a deep breath, and I step in again, though I know I am risking the wrath of Sam.

"Look, Sam, Rory's come down from… Exeter?" I look at Rory, who confirms this with a nod. "So he can't really go back home."

"So where's he staying tonight? Not with us!" Sam storms.

"Grandma said we could stay at her place," Sophie says. "Because they're going to be at Lydia's hotel."

So Karen knew he was coming! This does not bode well. I see Sam swallow.

"You're staying at Mum's? With him?"

"Mm-hmm." Sophie sees too late that she's given away too much too soon. "I was staying there tonight anyway, you knew that. I went straight there from the station, so all my stuff's there."

In all the excitement and stress, I don't suppose Sam or I had really thought of this. It had just been assumed Sophie would be staying at her room in our house. But she's right, she went straight to Karen's. I suspect this was very likely by design because with Karen and Ron at the Bay Hotel, she has the place to herself. Well, her and Rory.

"I'm going to kill Mum," Sam growls to me. I think I see fear on Sophie's face now, too. I try to smile and at the same time placate Sam.

"No, you're not," I say. "It is her wedding day, and didn't you give a speech earlier about how lovely it is to see her so happy?" I take his arm and guide him away. "Come on, let's go outside for a bit and talk this through. It might not be as bad as you think."

"Not as bad?" his words burst out of him. "My eighteen-year-old daughter sleeping with a… a… man!"

I think of Rory and again consider that he looks more like a youth to me than a man. Yes, he has some stubble, and he has a car, and he's twenty-five, but really, he's not a man in the same way that Sam is, or Luke, or Dad, or Ron. "He's not all that long out of his teens, really," I say gently, as we step outside, and the world softens around us.

"He's seven years older than her," Sam says.

"Well, yes, I know. You're right. But he's a young twenty-five. You can see it. And besides, like we said before, you can't do this. You can't react like this to Sophie's choices, because you will drive her away. And you may not like it, but this is Sophie's choice. Who she goes out with. Who she sleeps with…" I wince as I say this, grateful my expression will be hidden in the dark.

"Don't!" he says, but I can sense the anger draining from him.

We walk, holding hands, towards the shore. I can hear the fizzing and frothing of the gentle waves. The moon is hiding at the moment, behind a large cloud, and I can just see a vague glow in the sky.

For a while, we don't speak, but eventually Sam says, "I'm an idiot."

"No," I say. "You're not." And I mean it. "You are a concerned dad, and you're annoyed with Sophie for not asking if Rory could come, although apparently she has asked Karen instead, and she's said yes. You're annoyed with your mum for not telling us – which is fair enough. Being annoyed, I mean," I add hastily, in case he thinks I'm sticking up for his mum. "But I think, although this is a far from ideal situation, you've got to think it through, and act in the best interests of everyone, and especially in the best interests of Sophie. And your relationship with Sophie. You know, the chances are this won't last, and don't you want her to know that you'll be there for her if it doesn't? She won't want to do that if she thinks you'll just considered yourself vindicated."

"My god, you're a wise woman, Alice," he says, stopping and turning me by the shoulders so I'm facing him. "You are right, I know you're right."

"Yes. Of course I'm right." And I want to stay with him down here, cradled in the quiet of the beach at night, but

151

the band is playing once more, and the Beach Bar is glowing with light, and life, and in there are Sophie and Rory, and Karen, who despite her faults or – let's be generous – possible misjudgement, does deserve to enjoy her wedding day. "Come on," I say, "let's get back up there. You can buy Rory a drink."

"I don't know if I'll go that far," Sam says, "but I'd better try and find out what she sees in him. And what his intentions are."

This makes me laugh, and I squeeze his arm, walking happily back up the beach with him. Behind us, the moon breaks cover and lights a path across the sea.

22

At breakfast the following day, Sam can barely look at Rory. It was my idea to invite him and Sophie out, in the vain hope of producing some kind of positivity, but I think it may have been too soon.

"So, Rory, what are your plans over the summer?" I ask, trying not to sound like I'm grilling him.

"Well, I'll be working, of course."

Good. He sounds respectable.

"On my music, I mean."

"Oh yes?" Uh-oh. This does not sound like it's going to appeal to Sam.

"Yeah, I'm doing a collab with a guy in Bristol. Old school drum'n'bass, that kind of thing."

"Ooh, good. That sounds… interesting." Oh my god. I sound so old. There was a time when I would have loved to talk music with somebody like Rory. I get it, what Sophie sees in him. He's creative, a free spirit, and appealing to look at, with his curls and his freckles and his boyish smile. I get it, but I don't think Sam will. In fact, I know he doesn't. I am relieved when Luke, Julie and Zinnia appear through the doorway, which is so low that Luke has to bend his head down to get through.

It's a cosy café, Joe's, and it's stood the test of time. While many other cafes and restaurants, and even shops, have been passed through many pairs of hands over the years, Joe's is still Joe's – literally. And his smiling face is one of the best things about it, although the sea view and the non-extortionate prices are also very welcome. I remember coming here when I was Sophie's age, and Julie and I would have a cup of tea and a fried egg sandwich on a Sunday morning, after work. Then home for a snooze, and down to the beach.

The décor has barely changed since then, which is not to say the place is shabby – far from it. But it is down-to-earth, and unpretentious.

"Hey, you guys," Luke calls across from the counter. Julie smiles while Zinnia, who clocked us first, is already heading our way. It sends Ben scurrying out of his chair to give her a huge hug. An older couple seated nearby smile. I do, too. I have to take some of the credit for his cuteness, don't I?

Julie sits at the table next to us, and pulls Zinnia onto her knee while I settle Ben back in his chair and encourage him to drink his milk.

"How was the big day, then?" she asks. And her eyes fall on Rory. "And who's this?"

Sophie's boyfriend's cheeks flush. Whether it's from Julie's directness, or attention from an entirely gorgeous older woman, I don't know.

"This is Rory," Sophie, says, unfazed. "He came down last night, for the wedding reception."

"Hi, Rory," Julie reaches across to shake his hand. "So how was it?" she says, impatiently. "Everything go without a hitch? Isn't that weird? Getting hitched. Without a hitch. Never thought of that before."

I think we are all grateful for Julie's babbling.

"It was a lovely day," I say. "It did all go perfectly well, and Sam's speech was lovely. I think we all welled up at that."

"Did you make a speech, Mr Branvall?" Rory says, politely, and I have to hold the laughter in. I know Julie is doing the same.

"Call him Sam!" Sophie says, squeezing Rory's hand. "That's alright, isn't it, Dad?"

"Sure," Sam says, his voice a little gruff.

Luke comes across and sits heavily down opposite Julie. "Good day yesterday, was it?"

"It was lovely," I say, taking the lead again. "Thanks for looking after Meg as well. I hope she behaved herself."

"She was good as gold. We've been out for a good old yomp this morning, too, we left her snoozing away at home!"

"I was just saying about Sam's speech," I say, keen to keep conversation going. "It was lovely."

"Ah, well you're well practised, aren't you, Sammy? You did a cracking one for Julie and me. Be your turn next, eh, Soph?" Luke winks at Sophie. I can feel Sam practically crackling with tension.

"Hopefully not just yet," I say, smiling, hoping to defuse the situation. "So, how's things at Amethi?" I ask Julie.

"Amethi's their business. The place I was telling you about," Sophie tells Rory.

"Ah yeah, that sounds just my kind of place. Can I come up and see it sometime?" he asks.

"Of course. Maybe next time you're down…" I trail off, unsure how sound an idea it is to be inviting him for another visit.

"I was thinking I might stop around for a bit, actually. Hang out with Soph a bit, now she's down her for a while."

Silence. What do I say? Really, I want Sam to answer, but he's staying silent. I am sure his knuckles whiten around his coffee cup.

"Oh, right, well, I don't know… I'm not sure if we can squeeze anyone else in at the moment, at home I mean," I flounder. Sophie does have a double bed, but I really don't think I can invite him to share it with her.

"That's fine, I've got my tent in the car. There's that site just at the top of the hill, I was thinking I'll stop there, or find somewhere up along the cliffs."

"You can't just camp anywhere," Sam says, and I see Julie and Luke both clock the antagonism in his voice. They look a bit taken aback, actually. I can see Sophie is a bit upset, too.

"You can't, I'm afraid," I say. "You'll get moved along, most likely. But yes, that site's lovely – or there are a couple just a bit outside town." I can't look at Sam, as I'm sure he'll think I'm being a traitor, but really, what has Rory done to warrant such cold treatment?

"I'll check it out later," Rory says. "Thank you, Mrs Branvall."

"Alice," I say firmly. He smiles, and so does Sophie.

After breakfast, we head down to the beach with Luke and Julie. While Ben and Zinnia get stuck into digging the "biggest hole in the world", and Holly settles on my lap, Luke brings across some cups of tea from the café. He sits next to Julie and puts his arm around her. "Sophie and her chap gone back to your place?" he asks.

"They've gone to get their stuff from Karen's. They stayed there last night."

"Young love!" says Julie.

"Don't!" I nudge her.

"What? He seems nice."

"Sam doesn't think so."

"Really? What's the problem, Sam?"

"He's too old for her. And he's a layabout."

"A layabout?" Luke bursts out laughing. "Is that really you, Sammy? I don't think I've ever heard you say that about anyone. And half our friends were layabouts... some of them still are!"

"But they're not going out with Sophie," I say.

"How old is he?" Julie asks.

"He's twenty-five."

"Really? Doesn't seem it," she says, completely unshocked.

"You know who he reminds me of?" I say.

"Who?"

"Gabe. Your Gabe! I mean, not your Gabe anymore," I add quickly, but Luke laughs.

"Water under the bridge, Alice. Honestly!"

Gabe was Julie's fiancé, once upon a time. She had dumped him in a cowardly letter, and made me move down to Cornwall with her to escape. OK, that is simplifying things somewhat and I was more than happy to move down. I had my own issues to escape, for one thing. But he was a nice bloke. Just a bit... flimsy. Wishy-washy. An artist with a questionable work ethic. By the time he had realised that Julie wanted, or even needed, more, she had realised her feelings for Luke. I'd say she made the right decision, though I still have nothing against Gabe.

"It's tough, isn't it?" I muse. "We all love music. We love the arts, and we love books. And the people who make those things have often opted for a more alternative lifestyle, to make it happen. They've taken chances and risks, and probably gone without, because they believe in themselves, or at least in giving it their best shot. And where would we be if all our favourite bands had decided that actually they just needed to settle down and get a mortgage?"

"Yeah, but for all the people who take those risks, how many actually succeed? And how many are actually using it as an excuse not to get a real job, and sit round smoking weed instead?"

"Sam!" I say. I laugh, but I am a little bit shocked by his attitude. "Are you saying that's what Rory's doing? And are you saying that everyone has to settle for the same kind of life, all fitting neatly into the same shaped box?"

"No, I'm not, but there are plenty of us who do have to just get on with it. Earn a wage."

"Yes, there are." I can't deny that. "But didn't you take a chance, when you went off to uni? And what about Luke, starting his business, and me and Julie with Amethi? We all have taken risks, to make something happen in our lives."

"Yeah, but we weren't doing drum'n'bass *collabs* with some bloke in Bristol."

"Oh my god." I have to get up, he is driving me mad. "Come on, Holly, let's go for a paddle," I say.

She willingly comes along, although at the feel of the cold water on her pink little toes, she squeals, and I have to swoosh her up in my arms. I love the warmth of her soft cheek against my neck. I breathe in deeply; a combination of Holly and the sharp, salty air. I carry her along the shore for a little way, and back again, feeling calmer. I return to the group to find the conversation has moved on, and I'm grateful. But I still can't quite look at Sam yet. I don't want to see, if he's still edgy and angry. I don't like him being like that. He probably just needs a little bit of time, to accept the situation. By which time Sophie may well have moved on to somebody new anyway.

23

Two days later, I am in the office when my mobile begins to ring. It's David.

"Hi!" I say, glad to hear from him. "How are you?"

"Alice," he says, his voice muffled and broken. "It's Bob. He's died."

"He's what?" It takes me a moment to register what he's just said.

"He died. Bob died." He sobs now. He's done the hardest part, in saying the words out loud, and he cries long and hard.

I don't say a word, just hold the phone to my ear, while I let the news sink in. After a while, David goes quiet. I can just hear him breathing.

"What happened, David?" I ask gently. The last I had heard, all the signs were quite positive. And I feel bad, again, that I have not been in touch as much as I should have been. But Martin had told me Bob seemed pretty stable. He was strong, he said, and seemed to be through the worst. We have had so much going on, with the wedding, that I have let this strand of my life drop a little, and I feel awful.

"It was a shock, to be honest. He had been recovering, we thought. He'd been sitting up in bed, and he and Bea were on FaceTime once or twice a day. I spoke to him, too," David sobs again. "Just at the weekend. But he got an infection, I think, and he was still weak, and his body didn't fight it like it should have. They tried to treat it, but he died anyway."

"Oh my god. I am so, so sorry. How is Bea?" What a stupid question, I tell myself. How the hell do you think she is?

"She's broken, Alice. Broken."

I don't know what to say. I literally cannot think of any words. Or the ones I do think of are lame, and futile. Instead, David and I are silent, save for our breathing. Thousands of miles apart, and connected only by the flimsy, invisible, fragile internet.

It's nothing, I think angrily. This phone call is nothing. I am worthless and helpless and useless to David right now. And to Bea. I want to throw the phone at the wall. It's not fair. All the people who this virus has taken. All the lives it has ruined. It was not taken seriously enough soon enough, and it's broken us all. But some more than others.

"How is Martin?" I ask.

"I haven't been able to get hold of him. The kids are with his parents today, and he's in London at a meeting."

"Oh no, David."

"You're the first person I've told. I had to wait till Bea fell asleep. Crying and painkillers did it. Not too many painkillers," he says swiftly. "But I can't sleep. I'm looking out of their apartment window at the lights downtown, and I can even see the hospital all lit up, a few blocks away. It's huge, you know. Much bigger than the ones at home…" He trails off.

"How are you, David?" I ask now, quietly. I should have asked this first.

"I don't know!" He laughs. "He's not my husband, is he? It's Bea who's in mourning. Bea who's in shock. Bea whose whole life has been turned upside down."

"But you're in shock, too. And it still affects you. So don't belittle your own feelings, David, please." All of this is coming from nowhere, but I go with it. "You're going to be supporting Bea, I know. She will need you. But you will need support, too. Don't deny yourself the chance to grieve. I know you loved Bob, too." I stop, take a deep breath. "Sorry for the lecture!" I laugh lightly.

"It's appreciated. I mean it. It's just good to hear your voice."

"I'm here for you, whenever, David. I know you've got Martin, and I know he will look after you, but don't forget you have me, too."

"I won't."

"Go and get some rest now, if you can, OK?"

"OK."

"Or we can talk more if you want."

"No, no, it's fine. I don't think there's anything more to say right now. I just… I'm just glad I told you."

"I am, too. Love you, David."

"I love you, too."

It's a strange day. It's normal. I'm at work. Busy, as ever. Then it pops into my head: *Bob died.* Images of him come to me: when I first met him, when he and Bea were surprise Christmas guests at the Sail Loft. It could have been a nightmare. I was already frantic with nerves, but Bob was so lovely and laidback, and apologetic for not giving me warning. And Bea was so happy. She was glowing with happiness, and she's never lost that since. Well, not until now, of course. I feel her pain, sharp and deep in the pit of my stomach. To have found somebody who can make you so happy, to lose them in such a painful way. In any way. I can't bear it.

But then, as I say, the day becomes normal once more. A phone call; an email; a request from one of our guests to book a minibus for Thursday to take them to the Eden Project. Although it must feel to Bea like the world has ended, the day unfolds before me as it must, and soon enough, Julie is here. I tell her the news, and a lump sticks in my throat as I try to push back the tears. I feel nervous; an impostor, sharing somebody else's terrible tragedy as though it is my right to do so. As if it affects me in any way.

"That's awful," Julie says, her former smile fading away "Poor Bea."

"I know."

"What's she going to do?"

"I don't know."

"I suppose it's too soon for her to think about that."

"It's probably too soon to think about anything. And Bob has… had… kids too, didn't he? I hope that they're nice to Bea. I hope they stick together."

"At least David's still there."

"Yes, poor David as well."

We sink into silence for a while and I know we are both finding it hard to break it, especially with talk about work. It seems so inappropriate, to be thinking of anything other than Bea and Bob. But at the same time, we have paying guests here, and we need to keep things going for them.

"I know it seems trivial now," I say eventually, "but Mr

Robson has asked if you can pop across to see them, something about the fish for their dinner tomorrow…"

"Sure. I can do that," Julie laughs softly. "The show must go on!" She pulls herself up straight, and I try to do the same. "You get on home now," she says. "Will you see Martin tonight?"

"I might do, actually. Yes, that's a good idea. Maybe once the kids are in bed." The thought makes me feel slightly better. Martin is the best link to David and to Bea, and going to see him might make me feel a little more connected, and a little less useless.

Sam is home, with Holly and Ben, and he's got a pan of pasta on the go. Meg comes to greet me, her tail wagging her whole body, and I crouch to stroke her, pressing my face into her fur.

"How was your day?" calls Sam.

"OK thanks," I say. I haven't told him the news yet, as I didn't want to do it by phone, and certainly not a text. I go into the lounge and give Ben and Holly a cuddle each. They are sitting next to each other on the settee, little legs straight out in front of them, each with a plastic bowl of raisins. They are watching CBeebies, and consequently I don't get much of a look in.

In the kitchen, Sam turns and smiles. "What's wrong?" he asks, his smile fading in much the same way Julie's had.

"It's Bob," I say. "He died."

"Oh god." He comes towards me and hugs me. "What happened? I thought he was improving."

"So did I. David said he had an infection or something. I don't know."

"Oh god," he says again. "It's awful."

"I know."

It seems unreal. I feel shocked. And it's not like Bob was somebody I knew really, really well. But the stark reality of his death, and the fragility of life, has hit me hard.

"How was your day?" I ask, unconvincingly.

"Oh, fine," Sam says vaguely, his mind elsewhere.

"I thought I might try and see Martin later, if I can."

"Sure. Good idea."

"Oh, but he's in London," I remember.

"Maybe he'll be back by now?"

"Maybe. I'll message him and see."

As it turns out, Martin is due back later, and Tyler and Esme are staying at his parents' for the night. I pick him up from the station, and bring him back to us. He is in shock.

"Thanks so much for this, Alice. I couldn't bear to be alone tonight, and especially not at our place. It already feels so empty without David. God, I miss him."

"It's my pleasure. Our pleasure," I say. "Hopefully David'll be back soon."

"I hope so."

He is quiet all the way back to our place, but I feel like his spirits lift a little when we go through the front door. There is something about a lived-in home, I think, that can be so comforting. God knows it's far from tidy, but the little shoes by the front door; the children's coats hanging on their own low-down hooks. The lingering smells of a meal, and the innocent artwork on the fridge.

"In here!" Sam calls, semi-quietly, and we go through to the lounge to find him sitting on one of the armchairs, a bottle of wine open on the table, and three glasses. He holds one up questioningly to Martin.

"Yes, please, mate." Sam pours, and Martin gratefully accepts the glass, sitting heavily down on the settee. Sam pours another, handing it to me, and I sit on the other end of the seat to Martin.

When Sam has poured himself a glass, he raises it into the air. "To Bob."

"To Bob," we echo, and we each lift our glass in a toast to the lovely American who brought so much light into Bea's life.

It's a quiet evening, none of us talking much, but glad to be together.

"You're in Sophie's room," I say to Martin. "I hope that's OK."

"Where's Sophie going to sleep?"

"Oh, she's, erm, out for a couple of days."

A touchy subject. Sophie is camping with Rory. They've gone down to Sennen, which is not all that far away, and has a great beach for surfing – and a cafe that is Sophie's favourite. It's an extra sore topic for Sam as it's where he would always take her. I do feel a little bit sorry for him, being usurped (or at least it must feel that way to him), but I also think he's behaving like a bit of an idiot, and I feel that even more now that we are faced with this heavy news about Bob – life is far too short to be falling out with the people we love. And especially when really it is up to Sophie, who she goes out with. Her life. Her body. Her choice.

Will I feel quite as easy about things when it's Holly's turn, and Ben's? Do we feel more protective of our daughters than our sons? I don't suppose we should, but we know that girls are more vulnerable in some ways.

"With her boyfriend. Not that he's exactly a boy," mutters Sam.

"Oh?" I am grateful to Martin that he doesn't let on how I've already confided in him about Rory.

But with this fortunate segue, on an unfortunate topic, we hook onto something else to talk about, which takes our minds off Bob and Bea and David, for a little while at least. Martin is great, too, saying the same things to Sam that I have, but it feels like Sam listens better to him than to me.

"Just ride it out, Sam," Martin says. "Chances are, she'll get bored and find somebody new. And you don't want to push her away. Remember what it's like, when you're young and in love. And that feeling of being sure you are one hundred per cent right about everything. It's something to do with dopamine, and testing things out. She is still young, she is still learning. What you don't want is for her to come to the other side of this and find that you and she have been pushed apart by your disapproval. She needs you, and she always will."

"Thanks, Martin. I guess you're right."

I swallow back my indignation. Sam hasn't wanted to hear all this from me. He feels like I am taking her side, and he doesn't like the fact I don't agree with him on this.

"Trust me, Sam. Keep her close, and support her."

"OK. OK," Sam says softly. "I will do my best. It doesn't mean I have to like Rory, though."

"Of course not! But Sophie has to like you. And she won't, if you make life difficult for her."

When the bottle of wine is finished, we sit for a while, and eventually go to bed. It's a strange reluctance I feel, and I think we all share it. That marking the end of this day moves us a step away from Bob. At the start of the day, he was alive. Now he is gone. What a thought. But all of us have work tomorrow morning, and children to look after – a husband and a sister-in-law to support on Martin's part; a daughter to make amends with on Sam's. Life must go on.

24

I toss and turn all night, though. It's humid anyway, and even with the window open, there is so little breeze that the air stays still and thick and hot around us. Sam can feel me fidgeting, and in the end, when the birds have been singing for a good hour or so, and my eyes just won't stay shut, I tiptoe quietly downstairs.

Meg looks up, confused to see me here quite so early. Just like on the solstice, she's reluctant to leave her cosy bed, but as I put the kettle on and put some fruit from the bowl into my bag, she raises herself, stretching her front legs and yawning widely and noisily. I write a note, letting Sam know where I've gone, and telling Martin to help himself to some breakfast, and then I get Meg's lead and we leave through the back door, letting ourselves out of the side garden gate.

The streets are nearly empty – just the odd car passing by. Meg trots by my side, alert and eager now that we're out. The steep hill helps us keep pace, and it isn't long until we are down in the heart of the town, where we disturb a gang of seagulls who are busy pulling apart a bag of chips; it's so early that even the street sweeper has not been to do its rounds yet.

As we near the beach, Meg begins to pull at her lead, and I let her off on the slipway, smiling at the sight of her running down to the sand. I follow, pulling off my shoes.

The sand is cold on my skin. I call Meg, and we jog down to meet the sea, Meg barking and me exclaiming at the touch of the cold water.

We have the beach to ourselves, and I want to run across it. I want to shout. I feel a mess of emotions: sadness at what has happened to Bob, and Bea, running headlong into the elation of this rare feeling of freedom, and my endless love for this place.

I walk along with Meg, my feet becoming accustomed to the cold, and Meg dashing about, dashing pointlessly at the gulls, who wait and watch and lift into the air, swooping down and settling once more, further along. Meg has no chance. She knows it, they know it.

When we reach the rocks at the end, I turn, and now I see we are not alone. There is a figure further along, and I know immediately who it is. I want to wave, but I don't suppose he will know me from this distance. Instead, I walk towards him, calling Meg to make sure she's heading the same way.

"Craig," I say, when I'm close enough to the man that he can hear me.

His tall bulk was unmistakeable even from the far end of the beach, although today he is wearing an olive-green fleece, at odds to his usual brightly-coloured shirts. He turns, and his eyes take me in, and it seems to be a moment before he recognises me.

"Oh, hi Alice," he says, and at once there is a big smile on his face. But I am not fooled. The smile does not extend to his eyes.

"Are you OK?"

"Oh yes, love, I'm grand. I just couldn't sleep. So I came down here."

"Me too," I say. And I want to tell him why. I want to say that Bob has died. Like saying it will make me realise it is real. And like it will explain something about me. But I don't say a word.

"Thanks again for saving the day, on Ben's birthday," I say instead.

"That was my pleasure! He's a lovely boy. They were all smashing kids."

"They are, we're very lucky." I want to ask him if he has children, but I know very well that is not a question to ask somebody. Especially someone who appears to be very much alone.

"I came down to make peace with the sea," Craig volunteers. "I do it most days. She nearly had me," he laughs hollowly.

"It must have been terrifying." I stand next to him. We both look out across the waves.

"It was. It was. So stupid of me."

"Don't say that. It wasn't stupid. It was just… unfortunate."

"You're very kind," he turns and smiles at me. "It wasn't though, unfortunate, I mean. It was not… entirely accidental."

"Oh." I don't know what to say.

"I wasn't trying to top myself," he says quickly. "Not really. Not in any premeditated way. But I was there, and she was there, throwing herself against the walls and soaking me. I hadn't felt so alive for a long time, truth be told. I just thought, I'd see what came of it. Didn't think about anyone else. The lifeboat crew. Of course they'd come and save me. Put their own lives at risk. I didn't want that." He stops, and looks at me. "I'm sorry, I shouldn't be telling you all this."

"I think you probably should," I say gently, putting my hand on his arm. "I think you need to tell someone."

"I… well, I'm very sad, Alice. I'm alone. I'm in the place where I've longed to live all my life, but I'm alone. I lost my wife, two years ago. No. It sounds careless, to say I lost her. I was not careless, I cared for her deeply, but I couldn't save her. She died, and it broke my heart."

"I'm so sorry," I say, thinking these are sometimes some of the most futile words in the English language.

"Me too. She was a beauty. Gloria. We met late in life, compared to our friends. I'd given up thinking I'd ever get married, but then she came along. Met at a quiz, of all things. I was the quiz master! And it was her laugh that drew me to her. I'll never forget it. God, I miss her laugh."

I had not been expecting this, today. I had come here to shake off some of my own shock and my own grief, and I'd thought that I'd see nobody, talk to nobody, and get back home in time for breakfast. Now, I know time is ticking on. Meg is lying panting on the sand behind us, no doubt ready for breakfast herself, but I can't leave Craig now.

"Do you want to walk with us?" I ask. "I was just going to head back through town before work."

"No, no, you get on, love. And don't worry, I'm not about to do anything stupid."

"Honestly, you'd be very welcome," I say.

"Well… if you're sure."

"I am completely sure."

So we walk, and we talk, and I don't tell him anything about Bob. I like being able to listen to somebody else, although what Craig tells me makes me sad.

"I don't know if I'll stop down here, to be honest."

"That seems like a shame."

"I think it was a mistake. I don't think I've made a very good impression, and I've upset a lot of people… no, I know I have, Alice. And I understand it."

"But who? Who have you upset?"

"Well, you know, the ones at the meeting. I don't want to come and trample on people's toes, it's hard enough to make a living round here."

"But… well, yes, I understand that. I've felt the same myself. I don't know. We're lucky, Julie and I, to have been welcomed into the community, but it's taken a while, you know. And I think if you're willing to give back, people see this. And it makes it easier to integrate."

"I can see that," he says, treading heavily up the steps that take us up near the harbour. "And I'd happily do whatever I could, to help this town. Honestly, I've been coming here since I was a toddler, and I brought Gloria down here a few times. We got engaged right over there, would you believe." He points to the harbour wall. "We were looking out across the bay, and I hadn't planned it. It just happened. And she said yes!" He smiles for a moment, but while his mouth stays upturned, somehow his expression turns from happy to sad. "And just over there is where I was in June. When I… when the sea…"

The very end of the harbour, past the lighthouse and the lobster pots. I picture him standing there, alone, just willing the sea to do what it would.

"Oh, Craig. I don't know what to say."

"I know. I don't think there is anything anyone can say."

"But don't give up. Don't leave. Not yet. You said you'd

give yourself a year, and it's nowhere near that yet. You know, you've been through a lot, so you're not exactly starting here on an even footing. And it's always hard, to start somewhere new. Yes, there are some people around who make you feel unwelcome. But they're the few, I promise. It's just that they're the ones that shout the loudest. There are people like Diane…"

"Oh, Diane. She's a love."

"She really is."

"I've been helping her get her place back in order."

"So you are already giving something back!" I say.

"I suppose so."

"There's no suppose about it!" I don't quite know what's come over me, but I desperately want this man to be happy. He's big, but he's gentle, and he shines with kindness, behind the sorrow.

He laughs. "Quite the pep-talker, aren't you!"

"Yes. And you should know that I generally know what's best."

"I'll bear that in mind."

"But Craig, sorry, I am going to have to get home now."

"You go, my love. And thank you. You've given me a much-needed boost."

"I'm glad. Please don't just give up on life down here. I mean, it's up to you, of course. But give it a go. If you want to, I mean." I am suddenly aware of how bossy I perhaps sound. And that this is a man I barely know.

"I will," he says. "Or at the very least, I'll think about it."

"That sounds fair," I smile. "Have a good day, Craig."

"You too, love."

I have to walk fast to get back home in time, and I'm hot and sweaty by the time I get there. But the house is empty and there's a note from Sam:

Taken Martin home, and the kids to Mum's. I'll be late tonight, I'm going down to Sennen. See you later. Love you xxx

It makes me smile. I text him:
I hope you're not taking your gun down to Sennen.

When I get out of the shower, I see his reply: **No, I'm taking an olive branch, and a dove and a peace pipe.**

That sounds very good. Give my love to Sophie. And Rory xxx

I will. Did you have a good walk?

I did. It was lovely. Helped me get my head straight, a bit.

Good. Got to dash now. I'll see you later xxx

I do scrambled eggs for myself and for Meg, then we hurry into the car and up to Amethi. My mind is full of Bea and Bob and Craig and Gloria. Craig so desperate and confused that he tried to give himself to the sea. It didn't want him. It seems like life is not done with him yet, and I really hope he decides to stay.

25

When Sam returns that night, he looks tired, but happy. Relieved.

"How did it go?" I ask.

"It was good," he says.

"Did you see both of them?"

"Yep. But I went for a walk with Soph, and Rory made himself scarce. He's actually not too bad, I suppose."

I smile. "Such enthusiasm!"

"We had a good chat, though, me and Sophie, and I said I was sorry for being a dick."

"Did you actually say that?"

"No, not in so many words. But I did apologise, and then I took them both for tea."

"Did you? At the cafe?"

"Yes."

That really makes me smile. It feels like an act of generosity, for him to have shared that place with Rory. It's where Sam and Sophie have always gone together. "That's great. It's really nice. Was it very awkward, though?"

"No! Not really. I decided on the way over, I just need to think of him as being Sophie's age. I mean, he's still much closer to that than he is to our age. And he does seem like a kid, still."

"Well, he kind of is. He hasn't had to take on much in the

way of responsibility yet, has he? So he's still in that phase of life, where it's all about him. And now about Sophie, too."

"Yeah, I guess. Anyway, I said they could both stay here if they want to. There's not a lot of space in Sophie's room, but I'm sure they'll cope."

"That's a big step," I say.

"Do you mind?" he looks worried.

"No, I mean a big step for you, really, Sam. That's good. Sophie will appreciate it, I'm sure."

"How times change, though. Would your mum and dad have let me come and stay like that at Sophie's age?"

"Probably not," I acknowledge. "But you know, Sophie and Rory will find a way to be together if they want to. Better to keep her close, and let her know you appreciate she's growing up. She's a sensible girl, Sam."

"I know. God, I can't believe how grown-up she is." His eyes shine.

"You've helped her get to this point. You and Kate."

"And you," he says, putting his arm round me.

"And Isaac!" I add.

"Yep. This is the truly modern blended family, isn't it? Soph's got two parents, two step-parents, half-siblings on both sides... my god, we've put her through it, haven't we?"

"I don't see it like that. When I look at Sophie, I see a well-adjusted young woman who has a lot of people around her, who love her unconditionally. She might not have the traditional nuclear family, but in a way she has a lot more."

"Ever the optimist!" he smiles.

"I try." And I tell him now about Craig, and his sad story.

"Poor bloke," says Sam.

"I know."

"Will he stay, do you think?"

"I hope so. Or at least I hope he gives it a proper go before he makes a decision."

At the weekend, Sophie and Rory arrive. We put Rory's tent up in the garden, as to be honest there's not much room to store it indoors anyway. Holly and Ben love it, and they love Rory, too. He is energetic and happy to play with them, and that endears him to both Sam and me.

We invite Martin and the children over as well, which Martin is grateful for, but we are equally so. Having more people about dilutes the awkwardness of this brave new world we are facing.

"Will you go to Bob's funeral?" I ask.

"I don't think I can," says Martin. "I'd have to quarantine there, and then again back here. I just don't think I can do it. And I couldn't take the kids, anyway. It's too much for them. They're just settling in back here."

"How are they coping with everything?"

"They're alright, I think. I suspect death is a bit of an abstract concept, particularly to Esme, but they're both sad. They're happy to be back, though, and seeing their old friends again. And Mum and Dad, of course. Thank god Mum and Dad are here to help out."

"I know. We are so lucky. What would we do without our parents?"

"Even Karen?" Martin grins.

"Even Karen!"

She and Ron are so happy. It's a week already since their wedding, and they drop by in the evening, just after Martin, Esme and Tyler have left. They are doing the rounds, hand-delivering thank you cards for their wedding gifts, and they have left us till last.

"We had such a lovely time at the Bay!" Karen gushes. We are sitting in the garden, while Ron and Sam are looking at something on Ron's car. "Lydia wasn't there, of course, she was off with her young man. You know, the actor."

"Really? I didn't know that."

"No, well it's all hush-hush, of course, but you know what it's like when you work somewhere like that. Impossible to keep a secret."

"But you won't tell anyone else, will you, Karen?"

"Of course not!" she says, but I have a feeling from the way she answers that it's possible that ship has already sailed. I will have to catch up with Lydia and find out what's going on.

"Is it back to work on Monday, for Ron?"

"Yes. Oh, it's all gone so fast. I can't believe it's already a week ago."

"I remember that feeling." Our wedding plans had gone awry, when Sam had his accident, and we'd had to postpone everything. I remember watching the live stream of Shona and Paul getting married in our place, and feeling a bit sad, but really I was just so relieved that Sam was alright, it had altered my priorities.

Then Sam had sprung that surprise ceremony on me, and I hadn't been able to look forward to it, but the magic of that day stayed with me, and I remember that as time moved on, I didn't want to lose it. Gradually, of course, day-to-day life took over, as it must.

"I'm really tired, too," Karen says. "I think all the excitement's got to me." I notice the dark shadows beneath her eyes.

"Probably still getting over the hen do!" I laugh.

"Ah, maybe. Well, I won't be doing that again. But thank you, for organising it. I do know it's not your thing, really."

"I enjoyed it. Honestly. It was fun."

"I liked having that time with you and Janie. At the pool. That was the highlight for me."

"Me, too." And it's true. It was nice to see that softer side of Karen. It's even better to know she's so happy now. It's difficult not to contrast her happiness with Bea's heartbreak, but I know that always, when things are going well at any time, there are so many people out there whose worlds are falling apart. Likewise, when things are going badly, there will be other people having the time of their lives. I suppose we just have to grasp those good times and appreciate them as much as we can, and get our heads down, and grit our teeth, as we push through the bad times. As long as we remember that there will come a time that we'll reach the other side.

Karen and Ron stay until after the children have gone to bed, and darkness has descended. The night is still and warm, and we sit in the garden with the chimenea going, and the solar lights twinkling along the fences. Sophie and Rory stay with us the whole time, and I notice Rory make polite, interested conversation.

There is little from him, about his interests, beliefs, etc, and I suspect he's on his best behaviour. Whether Sophie has primed him to be so, or whether it's just how he is, I don't really mind.

That first evening, after Ron and Karen have gone, and it's

approaching bedtime, it does become a little bit awkward. The four of us are watching TV, but I can sense we're all tired. Nobody wants to make the first move. I bite the bullet. I yawn loudly.

"I'm shattered! I think I'll go up." I look at Sam.

"I'll join you," he takes the hint.

"Will you switch off the lights when you come up?" I say to Sophie.

"Of course." She looks at me gratefully.

"OK. Night, then."

Normally, Sophie will hug and kiss us both at bedtime, but I don't expect her to tonight. It's a lovely surprise when she does just this. I give her an extra squeeze.

"Goodnight, Rory," I smile at him.

"Night, mate," says Sam, and his semi-gruff tone makes me smile.

"Well done," I say, when we're up in our room.

"Don't patronise me!" he says, but he's smiling. And he turns on the radio, which he rarely does at night-time, but I suspect he's just trying to drown out the sounds of Sophie and Rory heading upstairs and into her room together.

26

"Mum's got covid," Sam says. "Ron, too."

"Shit."

"It's Tuesday night, and we've just got the children to bed. Sophie and Rory have gone down to the beach to do some evening surfing, and I'd been looking forward to an hour or two with the house to ourselves."

"She just got her PCR result."

"So when did she do the test?"

"Sunday."

"Sunday, the day after she was here?"

"Yes. She said she felt a bit ropey that day.'

"Great! So she came over to see us."

"I know." I can see he is worried about his mum, though.

"Never mind," I say quickly. "We sat outside all evening, didn't we?"

I always hate it when people's initial reaction to being told somebody is ill is self-interest ("Great, I wonder when I'll get ill now, then!"), but it does feel a little bit different when it comes to covid. We have tried so hard to be careful, and to do the right thing, for other people just as much as for ourselves.

"Is she very ill?"

"No, she says it just feels like a cold," he says.

"And Ron?" He is a little older than Karen, but Ron's so

active, he's probably healthier and more robust than most of us.

"He's about the same, I think."

"Let's hope it stays that way."

On Wednesday, I have a call from Mum. "Your dad's got covid," she says. She sounds very glum.

"Oh no. Honestly?" My stomach drops.

"I wouldn't joke about this, Alice," she snaps. I can tell she's worried.

"Is he OK?"

"Not great. Fluey, I'd say."

"And what about you?"

"I'm alright. And I've tested negative."

"Well, that's good. When do you think he got it…?" I ask, and I think… Karen! And Ron. They spent Saturday visiting everyone from the wedding, and giving out thank you cards. But really, what does it matter? It's not like anyone goes around spreading this on purpose… or at least, I hope not. And these days, the rules have relaxed, and we're meant to be getting back to normal. Or 'the new normal', as the irritating saying-makers have dubbed it.

"It could be from anywhere," Mum says. "Or could be one of our guests. Who now all have to do tests as well, and self-isolate."

"Oh no…" I say again. My mind is just catching up with the implications of this. Ten days' self-isolation. In a bed and breakfast. Will the guests have to stay put at the Sail Loft? Other bookings will have to be cancelled.

"I know. It is a total mess," says Mum.

"OK, OK, what can I do?"

"You can stay away!" she says. "Keep you and Sam and the children safe."

"OK… but there must be something we can do to help. So just let me know."

"I will. Thank you, love." Mum sounds marginally less stressed now.

"And remember, you're both vaccinated, so hopefully it won't be too bad. And maybe you won't get it at all."

"Yes, well your dad's isolating in our room, using our en suite, so he doesn't have to come out."

"Which means you've got the lounge to yourself… you can watch what you want on TV."

"True!" she does laugh now. "But I have to sleep on the little bed Ben uses when he comes over."

"Shame you can't use one of the guest rooms."

"I know. That would be much better. Never mind. Ten days sounds a long time, but after all those weeks of lockdown, it's nothing really, is it? Just as long as your dad doesn't get any worse."

"Fingers crossed. Give him my love, and tell him to phone for a chat whenever he feels like it."

"Will do, love. Will do."

"Dad's got it, too," I tell Sam. "Do you think we'd better test ourselves? Just in case?"

"I don't know. Have you got any symptoms?"

"No, I don't think so."

"Nor me. But maybe we'd better, just in case."

"I can't risk taking it to Amethi."

"No, of course, and I don't particularly want to spread it at the office, either."

Lateral flow tests it is. They make me gag, having to roll that thing on the back of my throat. Then they make me sneeze. It is far from pleasant, but it's not exactly a big deal in the scheme of things.

We initial our tests, and set the timer for fifteen minutes. Even so, I keep on checking, and am relieved to see both show a line only next to the C. Phew. Even so, it does feel like it is only a matter of time before we get it.

As the week passes, Mum too tests positive, as do half the guests at the Sail Loft. It presents them with a real problem. What do those guests who tested negative do? The rules are that if somebody in your household has covid, you self-isolate for ten days. But the Sail Loft is not exactly a household, and those people without covid are understandably keen to leave. Which they do. There is nothing Mum or Dad can do to stop them, and they wouldn't want to.

They are now, however, having to cancel all new bookings over the next ten days, and the people already there who are also in the grip of covid are staying put, till their isolation periods are over. A longer holiday, but not exactly in the vein they might have liked. At least some of them have sea views, I suppose.

"What about eating, Mum? What are you all doing?"

"We've got a little WhatsApp group going, to make sure we're all OK, and we're all mucking in to make each other cups of tea and coffee. It's quite nice, really. Well, maybe not nice, exactly, but it's a novelty. And everyone's pretty good-natured about it. Also, now that every one of us here already has covid, there is no need to isolate from each other, so we can use the dining room, living room, and even the garden, just as long as nobody else is in the vicinity."

"How weird, though!" I laugh. "It's a bit like Big Brother."

"Except hopefully we are not being filmed. I would not want anyone to see me looking like this!"

"Ah, poor Mum. Are you alright, really?"

"I think so. Your dad has definitely had it worse, but I think he's on the mend now, too."

My mind flicks to poor Bob. They had thought he was getting better. Then look what happened. Not that I expect the same thing to happen to Dad. It just makes me think. What a very strange illness. What a very strange time to be living through.

I have spoken to Bea, a couple of times. She's surprisingly clear and steady of voice, although, knowing Bea, perhaps it is not so surprising. She's been very used to making herself strong, and presenting a particular face to the world. But I know from David that she is crumbling, suffering insomnia, and then terrible dreams when she does sleep – and she's been having some issues with two of Bob's children as well, which must be awful. She must feel a long way from home.

"And I can't stay out here forever," David says. "I've had to book a flight back – Martin can't be on his own with the kids for much longer. I'm coming in September. And I can't wait. But I don't want to leave her, either."

"Why doesn't Bea just come back?"

"I think she will – if not with me, then soon after. But there's legal stuff to sort out here, as much as anything else. And I know she doesn't want to leave on bad terms with Bob's kids. Goddammit, they're not that far off my age, but they're behaving like total brats."

"I suppose their dad has just died."

"But Bea's husband has just died. They've all got families of their own. Bob was all Bea had."

"Apart from you."

"Well, yes, apart from me, and Martin and the kids," he concedes.

I hope Bea will come back to Cornwall. I don't suppose she is short of money, and she still has the flat here. There are tenants in at the moment, but I'm sure that she could even get a holiday rental for a few months over winter, until the rental agreement is up. Anyway, I suppose that's for Bea to sort out. But I'd like to see her. It feels very much that she is in the wrong place, now – and David certainly is. The children are missing him, and Martin is, too. As am I, although that is not quite as important.

So it seems that covid is still wreaking havoc across the world, despite many efforts to tell us it's over, and we can get back to normal. The new normal. Sometimes it feels like nothing will ever be normal again.

27

The next day, I wake up with a headache that painkillers are unable to shift, and I go to the home testing box (not quite as exciting as a pregnancy test). Lo and behold, there is the line next to the T, telling me what I think I knew anyway. I have covid.

"Bugger!" says Sam, from inside the kitchen. Ridiculously, I have stepped straight outside and away from my family, as a reaction to being in close proximity. I was in the same room as them only moments ago. But now I know, I know.

"I'll still have to do a PCR to be sure. You'd better all do tests as well," I say apologetically, as though it is somehow my fault.

"I could kill Mum!" Sam says, "And Ron."

"It's not their fault," I say, and he raises his eyebrows. "It's not!" I insist. "Honestly, they were just doing what everyone is doing – trying to get on with life."

"But they've always been so bloody-minded about covid. So self-centred."

"Yes, I know, but on this occasion, I really don't think they were doing anything that any one of us wouldn't do. And actually, we don't know for sure that it's come from them."

In the early days, it was like there was some kind of stigma and guilt attached to having covid. I remember our local Facebook page, which I spent far too much time on in the first stages of lockdown, full of chat about this virus, and whether anyone in town actually had it (there was still a lot of suspicion and disbelief as to whether it could really be as bad as they were saying) – and then when somebody was confirmed as having it, it was like their identity had to be protected. Of course, it shouldn't have been on Facebook, as that would be an invasion of privacy, but it was hardly something for them to feel ashamed about – I am sure that they probably felt bad enough, and possibly even terrified about what this new disease was going to do to them.

These days, with the vaccines, there is a lot less fear. And it's true to say that my first concern is not how ill I am going to get, but how this will affect everything else in my life, from Amethi to getting the kids to and from nursery, and even the logistics of living in the same house as two children, a teenager, a twenty-something we hardly even know, and of course Sam. This is not a big house. I can stay in my bedroom, of course, if nobody else has covid. Maybe Sam and the kids will be lucky and escape it. But with Sophie and Rory in Sophie's room, Sam's going to have to sleep in the lounge.

Ridiculously, I breathe in before I step back inside to go through the kitchen and hold my breath as I walk through. I head upstairs, go into our room, and shut the door.

Sam knocks on Sophie's door, and I hear him telling her the situation, and that she and Rory need to do tests as well.

"Is Alice OK?" It's Rory's voice I hear, and it makes me smile.

"I think so. Just feels a bit crappy. Thanks for asking, though," Sam responds, and I feel like the crack in his icy veneer becomes a little more defined.

The three of them head downstairs, and I sit on the bed and look at my phone. Who do I need to let know about this? Julie and Lizzie, of course. They are my first points of contact. Luckily, I have not spent much time with either of them in the last couple of days, and I think they'll be OK to go about their business as usual.

Then there are the guests at Amethi. I will have to tell them. I scan my memory for who I have seen and spoken to, and where. I don't think I have actually been in the houses, or that any one of them has been in the office with me. So we should be OK there, too.

I will have to get a PCR test to be sure, but I can't very well go in the car with Sam and the kids, or with Sophie and Rory. We will have to book separately. But I think it will only confirm what I already know. I open my bedroom door a crack. "Everything OK down there?" I call.

"Yep. All fine. All negative," calls Sophie. "Are you alright? Do you need anything?"

"No, I'm fine. Thank you, Sophie. I'm going to book my PCR test, Sam, and you'd better do yours and the kids' separately."

"We'll sort ours, too," Rory says. "Better to be safe than sorry."

That should be another brownie point for him with Sam, who I know will approve of this attitude. Maybe some good will come from all this. It's bloody annoying though, to say the least.

It only takes a day for the results to come in. Rory's and Sophie's come first, then Sam's and the kids', and then mine – even though I'd had my PCR first. Miraculously, it seems that everyone else has escaped the virus so far.

"Rory and I are thinking we might get out of the house while you're isolating, Alice," Sophie says from outside the bedroom door. "We've got the tent. We might go back down to Sennen."

"OK. Well, if you're sure. It might be sensible." The fewer people here, the better, I suppose. And Sam can have a proper bed, as well.

A little later, Sam calls goodbye to me, taking Ben and a crying Holly with him. My heart aches to be with them all, and I sink back into the pillows, feeling sorry for myself. I already miss them. I hear car doors being opened and closed, and the engine start up, and my family drive away to their normal days at nursery and work.

An hour or so later, Rory and Sophie shout goodbye to me, and they are gone, too, to the beach and long days of freedom. I envy them, but I feel no resentment. I've had those days myself. It's their turn.

Meg's claws click across the floor downstairs; I suppose she is heading to her bed. I think I will go into the garden with her in a while. But right now, I can't quite muster the energy. I'm already fed up of being forced into this isolated situation, although I know it is just a matter of days that I have to get through, and certainly nothing compared to what some people have to live with.

It's ironic, really; I regularly long for some time to myself. Now, I have exactly that, but not in any way that I had hoped – even fantasized – about. I now cannot wait to be well again, back in the heart of my family, and being run ragged by work.

As it happens, covid hits harder than I had expected it to. I fall asleep reading, and when I wake up I am hot and uncomfortable, then shortly afterwards I have that unique kind of cold that feels like it has seeped right into your bones and that there is nothing you can do to warm up – even though it's a hot summer day out there. And the breeze ruffling the curtains, the birds singing outside, reminding me what I'm missing. I need a drink, but I feel too cold and stiff and tired to move. Urgh.

There is a message from Sam on my phone, asking if I need anything.

I don't think I can move! I reply. **And I really need to drink, lots. And Meg needs to go out... xx**

Don't stress. I'm coming back. I can work from home while you're isolating xxx

I cannot express quite what a relief those words are. On top of feeling like absolute rubbish, I can't stop my mind whirring through all my responsibilities, and how to fulfil them, including giving Meg the attention and exercise she needs.

I must have drifted off again, as I wake to the sound of Sam calling my name, and Meg's welcoming bark.

"Hello?" I say. My voice is weak, like the lemon squash Grandma used to give me before she realised how much cordial to use.

I hear Sam's footsteps on the stairs. Such energy! I am envious, and I feel like I will never again bound up the stairs.

I know I'm being melodramatic, by the way. But it's how I feel right now.

"Are you OK in there?" I hear a little worry in his voice, and he knocks tentatively on the door.

"I'm OK," I croak pathetically.

"I've got you some supplies, and it looks like you've got a secret admirer, too."

"What?"

"Somebody's left some flowers for you. Here. I'll get it all together, and leave it outside your door, then retreat to a safe distance. OK?"

"OK." I am so grateful he's back, and so touched that somebody's brought me flowers, and so weak from this horrible illness, that I am close to tears. *Pull yourself together, Alice,* I tell myself. But I do feel better – safer – now that I know Sam is home. And I don't have to be on hand to answer the phone, or the door, or anything like that. I can just sink back into the pillows and relax...

I am just dozing off again when there is another knock on the door from Sam. It must only be about fifteen minutes later, and I can't seem to keep awake.

"There's soup out here," he says, "and bread, and those flowers. And a few more little things to keep you going."

I slowly roll myself out of bed and open the door. Sam is standing at the other end of the landing. This feels so ridiculous, not being able to be close, and I'd give anything right now to be able to just fall into his arms. But that would be incredibly selfish, even though I bet he'd let me.

Instead, I pick up the tray he's left me, which not only has soup and bread but a bag of butterscotch, a bar of Dairy Milk, and two cans of lemonade, alongside a box of paracetamols and another box, of tissues.

"Thank you," I say, involuntarily groaning as I take it through to the bedroom.

"You are in a bad way," he says.

"I'll be OK. Loads of people have it like this," I say. "I just need to sit it out."

I return for the flowers, and see they are from Julie and Luke. They are beautiful. I crouch to get them, and feel a bit light-headed, but I bring them into the bedroom, and I blow a kiss to Sam, then return to bed, just glad to be able to lie down again. I don't fancy the soup or the bread, or anything except sleep, in fact.

"Shout – or text – or whatever, if you need me," Sam says. "I'll be downstairs. I'll take Meg out later, before I get the kids. I'll let you know when."

"Great," I say. "Thank you, Sam."

And it's not long before my eyes are closing and I'm being safely welcomed back into the world of sleep again, where strange, vivid dreams await me.

The third day of my illness happens to be the same day as Bob's funeral, and although physically I am starting to regain my strength, emotionally I am all over the place. Well, quite honestly, I am more down than anything, so I am mostly in one place, and not a particularly good one. The fact that I am starting to feel a bit better only serves to make me feel guilty, in contrast to the pain that I know Bea, and David, and Bob's children, must be going through today. I have messaged both Bea and David, and received a heart symbol back from David, but nothing from Bea, which is completely understandable, of course.

The funeral is being live-streamed, which is another thing to come out of covid, or at least as far as I'm aware, it didn't really happen before then. I log in at the requisite time, feeling very strange, and very alone. I know Sam is working downstairs and can't log in. Martin, of course, is streaming it, too, and I'm so grateful to see his number flashing on my phone.

"Are you well enough for this, Alice?" he asks.

"Yes, of course."

"Well if you're sure, mind if we stay on this call, while it's happening? I don't want to be alone."

That makes me choke up. "Of course," I say, "I'd be really honoured to do that."

"Thank you, Alice."

"Can you see David?"

"No, not yet. I guess he'll be in one of the seats at the front."

The screen shows a few rows of heads, from behind, all spaced out to meet the social distancing requirement, and then a few empty chairs at the front. Soon enough, I see Bea and David, and two men and two women, who I assume are Bob's children and their partners, file in and fill the empty seats. At the sight of David and Bea, I catch my breath. I hear Martin sob. "Are you OK?" I whisper.

"Yep," he whispers back, resolutely.

It's like we are really there – hence the whispering, I suppose – and so throughout the service, we don't really talk. Not through the readings from Bob's sons, or the eulogy from Bea, which is heartbreakingly simple and reminiscent of her speech on their wedding day.

"Bob and I have only known each other a few years. And we met online, but I knew, from the first messages we exchanged, that he was somebody I'd like an awful lot. As it turned out, he was the love of my life. I've never been happier than I have in these last few years. I know to some of you, I am a newcomer here. An outsider, maybe – and some of you I have never even had a chance to meet. We were going to… we were planning to have a bit of a tour. I could meet Bob's family and friends, but we had those plans curtailed by covid. I just never imagined they'd be cut off forever. And now here you all are, but now I don't have Bob to introduce me, or give me context.

"When we met, I was maybe a little unsure. He seemed too good to be true. And I was scared to come out here and meet him for the first time, but my brother David said something to me, which stuck. He reminded me how our parents died far too young. And that life is far too short. He said time and tide wait for no man. He was right.

"Bob was the kindest, funniest man. And he loved you all, so much. His children, and their families. You meant the world to him." I see Bea's eyes go to Bob's family, and I can't see their reaction. I hope they are meeting her look, and sending her some support. I wish that we were there to do that for her. "And he wanted to come back here, and be with you. And I was happy to come. I'd have gone anywhere with him."

At this, Bea appears to collapse a little, under the weight of the day, and the weight of her words. David is by her side in moments, and ushering her back to her seat. I am touched as I hear a tentative clap, and then another, and then people are standing for her. It makes me feel she is not quite so alone.

When the funeral is over, the live stream ends abruptly,

and I am so glad to be connected to Martin. I think he feels the same.

"I don't know what to do now," I say.

"I know. That was weird, the way it just cut off. I suppose it had to."

"Yes. It's so harsh, though, isn't it? Such a horrible way to have a funeral."

"Such an awful way to say goodbye to somebody you love."

"I hope you're OK, Martin. I know that's a useless thing to say."

"It's not. There is nothing useful to say, anyway. Thank you for being with me, Alice."

"It was my pleasure. Well, not pleasure. You know…"

"I do. But you need to rest now. And I think I need to get out, get some fresh air. Sorry to rub it in," he laughs gently.

"No, you do that. Go out into the world. Enjoy it as much as you can."

"I will try."

When we've hung up, I am struck by how quiet it is, just for a few moments. It takes me back to that early lockdown, and I'd almost forgotten what it had been like. Then there's the loud putter-putter of a motorbike engine on the main road, and then a car, and another, and a neighbour dropping the lid on their bin, and the world comes to life once more.

For the rest of the day, I am exhausted. Probably I would have been anyway, but the funeral has definitely taken it out of me. I drift in and out of sleep, at times hot, at times cold, and my ankles and back ache, and I can't get comfortable. I have strange dreams, and I seem to keep revisiting Bob's funeral. In waking moments, I think I must contact Bea, and David, and I think of work I need to do, and I can't let my mind be quiet.

At some point in the late afternoon, Holly comes to the bedroom door and calls for me, and I hear Ben ushering her away, his big brother voice comforting and bossy at the same time. I don't say anything as I think that might just make things worse, but I desperately want to call them to me, and feel the definite warmth of their little bodies cuddled against mine. It makes me sad. Weak and ill, and lonely. But while my isolation is finite, and no doubt I'll be back in my life in days, all this behind me, Bea's loneliness is just beginning.

By the time Sam has gone to bed, I am wide awake. I don't feel quite so ill, but my mind is racing, and I can't push away the anxiety that has crept in. I just need to sleep. One good, clear, clean night's sleep, with no fever, no nausea, and preferably no thoughts. But tonight will not be that night. I turn on my bedside lamp, fish my book out from under my pillow, and hope to lose myself in somebody else's thoughts.

28

Mystery Woman makes Si Sigh

Oh my god! It's Lydia! I have ventured out of the house for the first time in nearly two weeks. I really was knocked for six by covid, and am only just now finding my feet again. It feels good to be out, and at the same time weird. A little bit like the first time venturing out after that first lockdown.

I double-take, to check I'm not mistaken. But no. Splashed across the front page of one of the tabloids is a picture of my former waitress, from the Sail Loft, now manager of the Bay Hotel. Lydia is looking beautiful in a bikini, next to a hotel pool somewhere distinctly un-Cornish; distinctly tropical-looking, in fact. Si Davey is laid out on a lounger behind her, with a small smile on his face.

It's been given equal space with the news of a hurricane in Haiti. I do sometimes think we have our priorities in a bit of a twist. Driven by a need to protect my friend – who is really only a handful of years younger than me, but towards whom I still have a feeling of maternal protection – I scoop up all the copies of this paper, and scan the racks for any others, but it seems the story is only running in the one for now. It may not be long before there are more, and before Lydia's identity is uncovered. Then who knows what?

Geraldine behind the counter gives me a strange look

when I dump my pile of purchases on the counter.

"My cousin's in there somewhere," I make up the lie on the spot. "Some interview about something, and I promised I'd buy as many copies as I could."

Geraldine just smiles, and rings the purchase through. Does she already know? She puts the papers into a thin bag, which does not look strong enough to hold all this weight, and the handles hurt my fingers as I walk out of the shop and down the road.

It's such a beautiful day, and I have been stuck inside for so long, I decide to take the road up out of town and cut back round to our house. I feel like I will be shattered by what seems such an exertion, when just a couple of weeks ago it would have been nothing.

At the top of the hill, I stop on a bench behind a wall and a thick hedgerow. Right down there, on the other side, is the sea. I can't see it, but I am grateful of the chance to rest, and to be honest it is just lovely to hear it. The constant, reassuring splash and thud of the waves below.

The sun is high up above my left shoulder, approaching its full midday height. It is August, and already I feel like September is in the air, with its traditional whiff of back to school, no matter how long it's been since I actually went to school myself. Soon, it will be Ben's turn to go – his first year at primary school. The thought makes me proud, and scared, and sad, and excited, all wrapped into one. I feel like I will miss these pre-school days, but the reality is that I work much of the time he will be in school anyway, and the difference it will make day-to-day is minimal. Still, it seems like a huge milestone, and the end of an era. But assuming we are some of the lucky ones, I know there will be many more eras to come, and these short few years from baby to school will seem just like a tiny drop in the ocean of Ben's life.

Taking a few moments to rest, and breathe, I practise the technique Lizzie taught me. I've been worried all along about the effect of covid on my lungs, but, despite feeling a little unused to the exercise, I think I am OK. I take the papers out of my bag, check the number referenced on the front page, and read the article in full. There are only a few lines. It's more photos, really. Lydia and Si 'stealing a kiss' in the pool. Lydia and Si sharing a huge cocktail with two straws. Sunglasses up on their heads. Smiling at each other. Lydia is called a 'redheaded beauty', and there is speculation as to whether she is a traditional fiery redhead – in terms of temper and also between the sheets. Oh god. It's so awful. I've always felt disdain for this type of sexist, pathetic reporting, but now, seeing it about somebody I know, I feel the full force of it. Lydia has parents; younger brothers; a great career (although I could well see Felicity rubbing her hands and capitalising on this publicity).

I don't know if Lydia is still away at the moment, but, imagining paparazzi waiting for her at the airport, I fish out my phone and call her. Straight to answerphone. Maybe she's already been tracked down and is having to avoid calls. I message her instead:

Lydia. You are probably already aware of this but you and Si are in the papers – or a paper, at least. Photos and all. I hope you're OK. Let me know if I can help in any way. Love Alice xxx

If I am very, very honest, there is a small part of me that is thrilled at the thought of Lydia with a famous celebrity. It's the part of me I'd like to deny existed. I would love to be lofty and rise above all this. I do know that Si is just a person, just like everybody else. He has parents, he used to be a baby, he almost certainly has to use the toilet like everybody else, and probably has his own range of problems and insecurities like everybody else as well. But also… it's Si Davey! I've seen him on TV, in films and series. He's even doing CBeebies Bedtime Story, if what I've read is true.

My phone buzzes. Lydia.

Alice. Thank you. I know. It's a bloody nightmare. We are on our way home now. I can't even tell you when or how I'm getting back. I'll be in touch, Love L xxx

OK. I am excited now. Why try to deny it? I sit back and smile at the thought of Lydia caught up in all this. She will be able to handle it, I hope. I think. The fact she's been away with Si tells me she does like him, more than she's been letting on. I just hope he is worthy of her.

Just as I'm typing a reply, my phone starts to ring. It's David. Seeing his name pulls me up short.

"Hi David, are you OK?"

"I am, thank you Alice. I'm fine. I have news. I'm coming home in two weeks!"

"You are? Oh David, that's fantastic." In my post-ill weakened state, it doesn't take much to bring me to tears and the thought of seeing my friend again does just that.

"There's more," he says. "Bea's coming too."

"Really?"

"Yes, really."

"Isn't that a bit soon?"

"No. She just wants to get home, Alice. She says she's got nothing to stay here for."

"What about Bob's kids?" I think back to the lovely words she spoke at the funeral.

"What about them? They're no good to Bea. Now Bob's gone, they don't want a bar of her. Never liked her in the first place, or so they say."

"That's awful."

"Yeah, well, I think it's all to do with money, really. And Bea doesn't want any of Bob's money. You know how proud she is. She says she just wants to cut her losses and get back to Cornwall."

"Oh, David."

"I know."

To cheer him up, I tell him about Lydia, then I feel guilty for gossiping, and I swear him to secrecy.

And once we've said our goodbyes, I sit for just a little longer. Tomorrow, I am back at work. I can't wait, but I know I need to take these last few moments of time to recuperate. And sitting here, on this bench, in the summer sun, I can't think of a better way to do it. A couple of hedge sparrows twitter in and out of the bushes in front of me. Landing on the lichened stone of the wall and eyeing me suspiciously before continuing on their way.

Eventually, a cloud crosses the sun, and the resulting shadow sends goose pimples across my skin. I stand, and spend a few moments just watching the sea. It's a calm day, and under the slightly clouded sky, the water is a darker blue, the way it is when night is moving in. There are paddleboarders out, and canoeists, and various boats, punctuating the waters for miles. I imagine being out there now, with just the sea for company. It's appealing, but then so is my home, and that's where I'm going now. To enjoy the freedom of the house once more, and another hour or two of quiet before life begins again in earnest. I'd better just put these papers in the recycling bin first.

29

I always feel like summers gain speed as they move along. Maybe it's to do with the times of the sunset and sunrise. The early days of summer are long, leisurely – lazy, even. The coming months stretch ahead, abundant with promise and life, as flowers begin to bloom, and baby birds begin to appear, fat with fluffy feathers, and frantically trying to catch their parents' attention.

I will wake with the dawn chorus but fall back to sleep, sometimes smiling, knowing that there are still a couple of hours' slumber before I have to get up and start the day.

As July turns to August, however, and the days are noticeably shorter, I feel just a hint of near-panic at the thought that we are approaching autumn. That the summer days and heat are diminishing, and it will soon be September, then October, and the clocks will change, and darkness descend. Which sounds like I hate winter; I don't, but I just love summer so much more. The ease with which we can leave the house; no need for hats, gloves, coats, scarves, umbrellas, boots. In summer, we can just slip on a pair of sandals, and we're good to go – even if it's raining. I don't mind wet feet when it's warm.

Now, in late August, that feeling of panic is exacerbated by the knowledge that in just a week or two, my little boy will be starting school. He's ready for it. But am I?

Thankfully, we have one last hurrah, as they say, to make the most of the final few days of the school summer break, and to welcome back some much-missed, much-loved friends.

David and Bea have been isolating since they've been back. Martin and the children have been staying at Martin's parents', but today they are returning home as the quarantine period is up, and, thankfully, neither Bea nor David has tested positive for covid.

"I'm convinced I'll never get it," David said on the phone. "Surely I would have done by now."

"Famous last words," I say, then regret the 'last words' bit, thinking of Bob.

"Like 'I wonder what this button does,'" David laughed.

"Exactly!"

"Anyway, Bea and I were wondering if there's any chance you and Julie and your assorted husbands and children could be free next weekend, for the bank holiday? I know it might be tricky, with work. But one of Bea's friends has offered us her amazing holiday lets, she's had a last-minute cancellation. There's loads of space there, and we thought it would be a fun thing to bring everyone together. Phil and Sue too, if they can, though I know it might be even more difficult for them."

"That sounds wonderful," I said. "I don't know, though. It could be tricky, as we've got a full house at Amethi. I'll have to see what's what there. Let me get back to you."

"Do your best, Alice! I need to see you! And we'll have a really good time. Something to lift Bea a bit, and help her forget things for a while."

"How is she?"

"Pretty terrible. And it's not helped, having to stay isolated from everyone for so long. I do think she's glad to be back in Cornwall, though."

"I can imagine. It doesn't sound like Bob's kids were making life easy for her."

"Understatement of the year. It's made me really angry, to be honest. And I just don't get it, how in the face of death people can be so shitty. They've all lost Bob. And the last thing he would have wanted was for them to be falling out."

"It's awful," I agreed.

"Well, Bea's made it very clear she's not interested in anything of Bob's materially, but he had stipulated a few things in the will, and legally his wishes have to be respected. Which is part of the problem. He's left her his house."

"Oh. Right. Which is why his kids aren't happy?"

"Yes. It's where they grew up, and lived with him and their mum. I suspect they've never really got over Bob and Miriam splitting up, even though she seems fine with it. Of everyone at the funeral, she was the most decent, in fact. She's even kept in touch with Bea since we've been here."

"She's not after the house, is she?" I am only half joking.

"Ha! No, I really don't think so. She's loaded. I think she genuinely cared for Bob, and is just a nice person. Maybe she feels like she has to compensate for her awful kids, too!"

I laughed. "Well, I'll speak to Julie about the weekend, and see what she thinks. Maybe we can work something out."

"I hope so, Alice. I really do."

Julie was very keen on the idea: "That sounds brilliant. It's a long time till our January break, and I could do with a little bit of a battery recharge."

"I feel a bit bad, having all that time off recently."

"That was for covid, Alice. I don't think that really counts as a break."

"I guess," I smiled. "I still feel guilty, though."

"Well, don't. You came back far too soon, anyway. You deserve a bit of time to chill, and get back on form as well."

"Are you saying I'm not on form?"

"That's exactly what I'm saying. You know it and I know it, Griffiths."

"Thanks very much!" I laughed.

"Any time. Now, at the moment, we've got a meal booked for the Higgins party, arriving on Saturday, and wanting a Saturday evening dinner. I could probably prepare it all, and freeze or fridge it, for Lizzie to put in the oven, if she's open to the idea."

"We can ask," I say. "I don't want her to think we're taking advantage."

"I really don't think she will, Alice. I think she enjoys it anyway, and it's a bit of extra cash for her."

It has made such a difference, having Lizzie at Amethi. I mean it when I say I don't want her to feel like we're taking advantage, but having a third reliable person on the team has taken some of the heat off Julie and me. It's all very well thinking you can have a family and run a business and have a life and keep a relationship alive, but eventually you will wear yourself out. And there are always unforeseen things that are impossible to plan for, especially with the number of bugs the kids pick up at nursery. I smile at my naivety when I remember being pregnant with Ben, and how in my head I'd still be working exactly the same way, just with a baby strapped to my chest, or sleeping in a cot next to my desk. As if it could ever be that easy! Having Lizzie on the team – and her being so easy-going and adaptable – has relieved some of the pressure.

And, true to form, she is very happy to be left in charge for the weekend. "Sounds like Bea will need you guys to give her a bit of a boost. And David, too. What a rough time they've had."

"Are you sure, though?"

"Yes… you can unfurrow that brow, Alice, and get packing! You'll only be an hour or two away if there's an emergency… but there won't be," she adds. "Go on, have a proper break – no, time off for covid was not a break," she pre-empts me, "and your body could probably do with a bit of time to catch up and recover properly."

"Lizzie, you are an angel."

"If I believed in angels, I'd agree with you."

"Well, whatever you are, I am very grateful."

And so it is that on Friday afternoon, I am heading home from Amethi with a huge smile on my face. I've said goodbye to the people who have been staying with us this week, and I've made double, triple, sure that everything is in order for tomorrow. Lizzie is primed to work with Cindy in getting the places in order for the new influx of guests, and Julie has prepared the Higgins' meal for Saturday night, and a last-minute request for a Friday night meal for the newly-married couple who have been with us this week. They've had yoga sessions from Lizzie every morning, and have hiked every day. I don't think their car has moved since they've been here. Tonight, they've clearly decided to treat themselves, and Julie is cooking up a seafood platter for them, followed by a summer fruit pudding and cream.

I have left Julie in the kitchen, putting the finishing touches to these dishes, and I'm collecting Zinnia from nursery alongside my two. Sam and I will bring Zinnia to the holiday cottage, and Luke and Julie will meet us there later. Between us, as we nearly always do, we've found a way to make it work.

I collect Holly first, then Ben and Zinnia. She has just recently joined the top room at nursery, and I'm struck by the difference between this room and Holly's. How grown-up these children seem, even though in reality they are so little. I know that once Ben is at school, he'll seem tiny again.

He greets his sister with a hug, which makes me smile, and then he and Zinnia hold a hand each of Holly's, and I take them out to the car, strapping them all into their respective seats. I have had to put Ben's seat in the front, which he loves. I don't fancy having to squeeze in between Holly and Zinnia for the journey this evening, but I am sure Sam's going to want to drive – and to be honest, I would take being squashed over having to navigate the tight Cornish lanes which David has warned us we will have to do, to get to the place where we're staying.

We head back home, where I make snacks for all, and play with Meg in the garden. She joins the kids on the settee for *Hey Duggee* while I pack the boot of the car. Luke and Julie have some of our luggage, in exchange for us having their daughter, so it doesn't take too long. Even so, there are bags of nappies, food, drink, swimming things, towels, soft toys, books, medicines and first aid kits (just in case), and Meg's crate to fit in. The boot is piled high, but I manage to get it to close, and I stand back for a moment, admiring my handiwork. Then I head inside for a cup of tea and sit impatiently waiting for Sam to return.

"We're already packed!" I say, excitedly, as soon as he is through the door.

"Good work, Griffiths. Can I just get a shower before we go?"

"Can you have one there?" I ask, pleadingly. "I just can't wait to go."

"I can see that!" he laughs, and kisses me. "Kids, who's more excited about this weekend? You or your mum?"

"Mummy!" Ben says without any hesitation.

"I just want to see David, and Bea," I say apologetically.

"I know!" Sam laughs. "Come on, let's get on our way, then."

"Thank you."

We strap the children back into their seats in the car, and Meg reluctantly gets into her crate. With a last check of windows and doors, I lock up, then somehow manage to squeeze past Holly, and take my place in the centre of the back seat. On the way out of town, we pass Karen and Ron, who are walking hand-in-hand. "They're so romantic!" I say. Sam makes a pretend-sick noise but he beeps the horn and they turn and wave.

Soon enough, we're on the A30, which slices through the land, and heading north to our holiday. It may only be three days, but the fact that it's such a short break might just make us appreciate each day that little bit more.

30

There are tears and hugs, and more tears and more hugs, when I am finally reunited with my friend. David is the closest thing I have to a brother.

"My god, I've missed you!" he says.

"The feeling is mutual," I say, wiping away a tear. I am nearly shaking.

Sam is standing back a couple of feet, holding Holly, who looks very shy. She's never even met David before, and it's possibly quite confusing for her to see her mum crying and hugging this strange man.

"Here, Holly," I say. "It's your uncle David."

Sam steps forward and, still holding Holly, hugs David, too. "It's good to see you again, David."

"You too, Sam. It feels like no time at all now. I feel like I've never been away!" David is laughing through his tears, and I can feel relief emanating from him. Now is not the time to get into the deep stuff, though. Esme and Tyler have appeared, and already requisitioned Zinnia and Ben, who run ahead of us up the spiral stairs, past the bedrooms on the floor above, to the top floor, where there is an open-plan kitchen, dining and living area - and a balcony with a hot tub.

Bea stands to greet us. She looks well. But she looks thin. And she looks tired, I see, as I get closer to her, and wrap her in a hug. I can feel a little sob rack her. "Hi Bea," I say softly.

"Alice," she says, and I hold her tightly, for as long as I feel her arms around me, and her face against my shoulder. It's a strange exchange of positions, as I've always felt a step behind her. Younger, less experienced, more naïve. She has taught me a lot over the years, but now it is me who needs to support her.

As her grip loosens, I step back, and see her eyes are glistening.

"It is so good to be back," she says.

"I bet."

"It almost feels like these last few years have just been a dream. Like I've imagined them. But come on," she shakes her head. "Let's get you a drink."

"I wouldn't say no."

"Sam, hi," she says, as he appears at the top of the stairs. "And this must be Holly?"

I smile as my daughter buries her head into Sam's shoulder. Ben is the exact opposite, dashing around the top of the staircase, followed by Zinnia, Esme and Tyler – or perhaps he's following them. It's hard to tell. "Careful, you lot," I say, "you're making me dizzy."

"Yes, just calm down, Tyler," Martin says, coming in from the balcony and kissing me on the cheek, then shaking Sam's hand. "You're the big boy, you've got to set a good example."

"Maybe we should head down to the beach in a bit," David suggests. "Let them wear themselves out. Then pizza for tea!"

The kids cheer, and Bea gets some bottles of beer and

cider out of the fridge. She opens them up, setting them on the side and putting out glasses so we can help ourselves. I pour some cider into a glass, and take a sip. The sharp fruitiness hits the back of my throat and, wandering out onto the balcony, I feel almost instantly relaxed.

Across a gravelled courtyard complete with a huge driftwood sculpture, I can see the sea dancing prettily under the late summer sun. Bea follows me out, and Sam and Holly, and we each take a seat, and a few moments to just settle. Inside, I can hear David and Martin playing a game with the four older children. Holly gradually turns herself around and settles on Sam, wrapping a section of his t-shirt around her thumb.

"This place is beautiful," I say.

"It's pretty special," Bea agrees. "I'd never been here before, or even to this bit of coast, or at least not that I remember."

"Up North," Sam laughs.

"That's it!" Bea smiles.

We are close to the Tamar Bridge, so not far from Devon, really. To most of the UK, this is still very much the South. I like the thought that Bea considers it otherwise. It reinforces my feeling that where she is from – where I live now – is somewhere else altogether.

"Thanks for coming," Bea says. "It means a lot to me."

"Thanks for inviting us!" says Sam. "Honestly, it's definitely us who should be thanking you."

Holly is watching Bea intently. I would love to know what she's thinking.

"We're really touched you asked us, Bea," I say. "Mum and Dad were, too. They were sorry not to be able to come.

But you know what it's like on the bank holiday weekend. And to be honest, Dad is still not fully recovered, from covid," I finish the sentence wishing I hadn't brought it up, but not wanting to shrink away from it, either.

"Is he alright?" Bea looks concerned.

"Yes, he's just struggling a bit, I suppose. Gets short of breath easily – and very tired."

"What a god-awful illness," she says. "Did your mum have it as well, Sam?"

"Yes, and Ron, but," he looks almost embarrassed, "they didn't get too ill, really."

I think of Karen, and how she has never believed in covid. Not really. How she didn't want the restrictions that were put in place, and didn't really want the vaccine, though she had it after a bit of pressure from Sam. And now, she's had covid and it barely touched her, or Ron, which has only served to reinforce her belief that she was right all along.

I try not to dwell on it, though, and when she and Bea meet again, I will at all costs try to avoid the subject, because I don't think that is a conversation that would go very well.

"That's great," Bea says generously, and sincerely. "I felt pretty sick with it, but I'm lucky not to have any long-lasting symptoms like it sounds Phil has. It's impossible to know how it will pan out, with it being such a new illness."

"It's a nightmare," I say. "A total nightmare. I just hope there aren't any more lockdowns."

"I just hope it's over soon," says Bea.

"I'll drink to that," says Sam.

We all raise our glasses together. I want to toast Bob, too, but I think that would be presumptuous, and maybe this is not the right time. But his absence is very present, and I feel like he is here with us; his tall, handsome figure always at the periphery of my vision. Just out of sight.

When Julie and Luke have arrived, and had a drink too, we all head down to the beach. It is literally two minutes' walk away, and it's almost entirely empty. At the far end is a small group of teenagers, which makes Julie and me smile – sitting around a fire and playing music – but aside from them, it is just us.

The steep slope down to the beach has a row of upended boats and boards locked up securely, ready to be freed and taken onto the waves by their owners. At the bottom of the slope is a curled harbour, the sea-facing wall partially broken away, and one lone fishing boat bobbing on the incoming waves.

We walk past the harbour and onto the open expanse of beach, Sam and Luke throwing a ball to each other, as Meg runs up and down between them, barking and determined that she'll make the next catch. David and Martin hold hands, and the three little girls walk together, stooping to look at shells and pebbles, while Ben and Tyler are racing each other across to the rock pools.

Julie, Bea and I walk companionably together, Bea in the middle. I feel like protecting her, and I guess Julie feels the same.

"How are you, Bea?" I ask. "I'm so sorry. About Bob."

She turns her head slightly and smiles. "Thank you, Alice. For saying his name. You wouldn't believe how many people seem to try not to."

"Do you think people just don't know what to say?" asks Julie. "Luke thinks that, about when his mum died. There were people who stuck by him, and there were people who just vanished, he says. To think that, when he needed them most – they left him, out of embarrassment at not having the right words!" She tuts. "What a stupid, repressed country this is!"

Bea links her arms in ours. "Maybe it's not just this country," she says. "Maybe it's just people."

"But we're all going to go through it, one way or another," Julie says vehemently. "Why don't we just talk about it? Sorry, Bea," she says, shamefaced. "We should be talking about you, and about Bob."

"That's fine!" Bea says. "And I agree with you. I remember that when Mum and Dad died; my social circle shrunk. And people were there at the beginning, but soon they forgot to ask how I was. Or forgot that I might be feeling different. It didn't help that my husband was such a dickhead!" I feel like we are all pleased to be able to laugh at this. "But it made me see things clearly, I suppose. And I hated that people weren't willing to talk about death. Bob was always very straight down the line about it. His parents had died, too. And his best friend, when they were a lot younger. He never shied away from it. He was a good man. A great man."

We stop. "He was," I say. "He was lovely."

"And so bloody handsome," Julie ventures. I can tell she's wondering if she should have said that.

Luckily, Bea takes this in good humour, too. "He was that," she says, smiling. "It's strange," she continues, and we sit, almost as one, side by side on the sand, "how it is when somebody dies. It's the worst thing in the world. The very worst. And I know that it's real, and that Bob has gone, but there is some small part of my mind that thinks once I've finally got through this horrendous time, he'll be waiting on the other side of it for me, and I can tell him all about it. It doesn't make sense, I know. But he's in my mind. He's my rock. When anything bad has happened in these last few years, I've known he'll be there. So it makes sense in my irrational mind that he will be there for me through this as well. Does that make any sense at all?"

"I think so," I say, trying to imagine what it would be like if Sam died. Knowing that whenever I need him, I am always secure in the knowledge that I have him to lean on, and to talk to. For Bea, Bob's loss is the very thing she needs him to support her through. He is the person she needs the most.

"Well, I'm not the first person to go through this," Bea says. "And I won't be the last. And people do get through it, I know. It will just take time. A lot of time."

Julie and I remain quiet. I really can't think of what to say.

"But I am glad to be back, girls. So glad. It was almost worth Bob's kids being so bloody awful, for the relief of being back here. And then having to quarantine – that was tough, but now life feels better. Because I'm out of the States, and I'm out of quarantine. Losing Bob was the absolute worst thing that could have happened, but then more bad things happened, and now they're over, I feel like life has improved a little bit."

"Well, I suppose that's a good way to look at it!" I say, feeling futile.

"It is," says Julie. "I think I can speak for Alice and me, that we don't really know what to say, Bea. Or we know that whatever we say won't be helpful or useful, or make anything better. But we are also not going to disappear, and we're so glad you're back. You and David. This is home, Bea," she says firmly, and I smile. It is not often that Julie waxes lyrical. She normally leaves it to me to witter on at people. "This is your home, and we're your friends. Your family. We'll never replace Bob, and we would never want to. But we love you, and we are here for you, and that is not going to change."

"Oh Julie," Bea says, and I feel she is shaking a little. She leans into Julie, and hugs her, and Julie holds her head lightly while she cries. All of the others are off at the other end of the beach now, past the small group of teenagers, whose freedom I envy. But then, they have had to go through something I never did at their age. They've been locked down in their homes – away from friends, away from school – for months at a time. I sincerely hope that they can now enjoy their freedom, and their youth, and I hope it is a very long time before they have to go through anything like what Bea is suffering now.

The rest of the weekend is nothing short of joyful. There are moments of emotion, of course – and quite a few, at that. But by and large, there is laughter, and such an overwhelming feeling of happiness at being together. Martin and David have missed each other terribly of course, and Esme and Tyler have also been missing their dad. To see their family reunited is wonderful and it's hard not to share their happiness.

I just wonder whether it might hit Bea even harder, her solitude, at being with three families, and heading off to bed on her own every night while we go off in our pairs. But I remember what she said about people not talking about things, and avoiding topics because they are awkward, and so I ask her straight out.

"Honestly, Alice, no. I don't feel like that. It doesn't make me miss Bob any more than I already do. And I feel a little bit less lonely, knowing that you are all around me anyway. Besides which, Esme's been sneaking into my bed in the middle of the night!"

"Has she?" I laugh.

"Yes, but don't tell David, he's been trying to train her into staying in her own bed, and he thinks he's succeeded! I don't want to ruin the magic for him!"

On the last day, we decide to make the most of the astonishingly quiet beach before we head home. The cars packed, save for our swimming things and buckets and spades, we spend a few happy hours on the grainy sand, the kids working together to create a sea wall to protect us all, while I go for a swim with Sam. The tide is on its way back in, and we walk hand-in-hand through the shallows and into the gradually deepening water.

"Feeling better?" he asks me.

"Do you know what? I really am," I say, turning and taking his other hand in my spare one. He leans forward and kisses me. With the water about waist-height, I snake my arms around his neck and return the kiss. I feel like I haven't really consciously thought about him this weekend. We've been all bundled up in the group, and keeping an eye on the children. It's nice to share this moment with just him, and feel his solid presence.

"I wish we could stay another night," he says. "Just me and you."

"That really would be lovely." I look into his eyes, and I smile. But already, I can feel reality pressing in on me just a little, and my mind turning reluctantly to the week ahead. To work. To school, for Ben. His very first day. There are shoes to be bought, and name labels; a lunchbox, and PE kit. By this time next week, Ben will be facing his first full week at school, and we'll already have jumped the hurdle of his first day.

We swim for a little while, Sam and I, heading out over the subtle waves, then returning to shore, to the warm group of friends and family who are gathered there. After crunchy, sandy sandwiches, it's time to get going. We walk barefoot up the slope, and it's only once we have waved off the others that I realise Ben's bucket still holds a small, juvenile crab.

"Oh no!" I say. "I'll have to take it back."

It's a nice excuse, really, to have a moment or two to myself, and appreciate the weekend, and this beautiful place. I walk down the now-familiar slope and, rather than turning right towards the beach, I turn left, lowering myself onto the sea wall and then the rocks below, where rock pools glimmer. I empty the bucket into one of the pools, and see the crab sink to the sandy bottom. In the clear, salty water, the creature stretches its legs. It's far from home now, I think, not knowing exactly where Ben will have got it from. Will it matter to the crab?

I sit on the sun-warmed rock and watch for a few moments, as the incoming sea gently pushes against the crab, rocking it. I hope it finds its feet, and finds its way to where it needs to be.

I turn and climb back up onto the path, trudge my way back up to the top, to the car where my family await me. I feel like this weekend has been a fulfilment of summer's promise, and that we can head on into autumn now, knowing we have done this season justice. New adventures await us, and I think of Bea's words from Bob's funeral.

Time and tide wait for no man.

I had looked up that saying, later. I'd heard it before, many times, of course, but never given it all that much thought. The internet informed me that the saying is sometimes attributed to Geoffrey Chaucer, but it is also said to have come from a Saint Marher, in the 13th century – or possibly it was around even before then. While the generally accepted meaning is not to procrastinate; to make a decision, and act, I also like to think there is something in it about life itself. That it moves on, always, no matter what is happening in your own little world – good or bad. It must have felt to Bea like her world ended when Bob died, but even at that very moment, other worlds were just beginning. A baby taking its first breath. A teenage girl preparing for her first date. The first line of a novel being written. There is no stopping time, and no preventing life from going on. We might try to swim against it, but that won't work forever. Maybe it's better to go with it, like that little crab, and trust that it takes us in the right direction.

31

A lovely surprise awaits us when we get back. Sophie! Sitting in the lounge, her feet up, and a cup of tea on the table next to her.

"What are you doing here?" Sam exclaims.

"You could sound a bit more pleased to see me!" she laughs, while Holly clambers on to her lap, and Ben (about to start big school, in case you're interested), maintains a cool demeanour for a few seconds, before leaping onto his big sister.

"Careful!" she winces.

"Are you OK, Sophie?"

"Oh, yeah, just a twinge in my back. Living in a tent will do that for you," she smiles.

"But why are you here?" Sam presses. "I thought you and Rory were living it up in Devon." I know this man. He's angling for some info. He's hoping they've split up.

"Yeah, we were, but Rory's gone up to his parents' for a bit, and I thought I'd better come and see you lot… especially this one, before he starts school." She tickles Ben, and he giggles uncontrollably.

Bad luck, Sam, I think. *They're still together.* I picture a future with Rory very much in it. It wouldn't be too bad. I quite like him, really. It's just he fits into a strange place, between our ages. He's seven years older than Sophie, but only about twelve years younger than me and Sam. It is a bit odd. But it could be much worse. I remember a girl at sixth form, who had an affair with one of the teachers. It was outrageous, really, though at the time we didn't see the whole picture. It seemed kind of cool – he was a young(ish) English teacher. He was probably about thirty, while she was Sophie's age – eighteen. He was good-looking and engaging, and it was a not-very-well-kept secret whilst we were still studying – then the secret came out shortly after our exam results. Julie and I, and many of our friends, were staunchly pro the relationship. Philippa was a young woman, who could make up her own mind. He wasn't married or anything like that. They were free to choose.

Only now that I am older do I see it differently. What must her parents have felt? They had entrusted their daughter's education and wellbeing to the school, only to discover that one of the adults who was responsible for these things was actually engaged in a romantic, and, let's face it – sexual – relationship with her.

But, to give them their due, the couple carried on – he leaving his job and becoming a copywriter in an ad agency, and she going to university as planned. They stayed together throughout. It was only five years later that she ended it – perhaps finding the mid-thirties office worker less attractive and appealing than the enigmatic, energetic teacher who had turned her head.

I make a mental note to tell Sam this story; maybe make him see that Sophie's situation is not really all that bad.

Except, before I get the chance to tell him, I discover that it is. Or at the very least, it might be.

When I get Meg ready for a late afternoon walk, Sophie says, "Can I come with you, Alice? I want to get a couple of things from town."

"Of course!" I say. "I'd love to have your company."

She is quiet on the way down the hill, though, and I begin to realise that all is not as it should be.

"Everything alright?" I ask.

"Yeah… fine…" she replies, unconvincingly. "Well, no, not really."

I can hear them there, in the back of her throat. The tears. I stop, and put my hand on her arm, to make her stop, too. She looks at me, and I see the tears are in her eyes as well.

"What is it?" I ask, with a sudden, strong feeling that I know exactly what it is.

"Not here," she says, looking around her. I know what she means. This is one of those towns where everyone knows everyone, which is lovely in so many ways, but not always what is wanted.

Heads down, we press on towards the surfing beach; an unspoken decision from us both. Once on the slipway, I let Meg off her lead and I take off my trainers, noting that Sophie doesn't stop to think of this. She walks headlong into the blasts of wind that shoot across from the sea. Now, the tears in her eyes could be a result of the wind, or the sand, as much as whatever dilemma she faces. As we walk along, Meg racing ahead, the words tumble out of her, confirming my suspicion.

"I'm… I might be pregnant," she says. And I sense it is a small relief to have said those words out loud.

"Oh Sophie," I say.

And I hope that the words don't come across as disappointment, because that is not how they are meant.

"I know," she gulps. "I'm so stupid." She screws up her eyes, as if willing the reality away.

I cultivate my question. *What happened?* won't cut it. The answer to that is fairly obvious. *Is it Rory's?* is potentially insulting. To me, my next words aren't really the point. I just want to move us on to where she is, what she wants to do, who knows, and where do we go from here.

I sit down suddenly, taking her hand gently, and pulling her down next to me. I put my arm around her, and she leans against me. I choose to say nothing for the moment. And I feel her body heave slightly with reluctant sobs. I hope that she feels comforted and supported. Keeping an eye on Meg, I decide I will leave it to Sophie to speak next. And eventually, she does.

"I'm not sure I definitely am," she says, pulling away slightly so she can look me in the eyes. "We're careful… you know… I don't want you to think I'm some unreliable, silly little girl, or that Rory's one of those blokes…"

"I know, I know," I soothe. I do know what she means. "Sometimes things go wrong," I say. "Nothing's 100% reliable. Well, apart from not having sex!"

I can't believe I've just said that. But to Sophie's credit, it makes her laugh.

"Have you told your mum?" I ask, wondering what Kate will make of this. Sophie shakes her head.

"Rory?" I suggest.

"Nope. Just you."

I can't help but feel a tiny swell of pride that she has entrusted me with this, but I know that is really beside the point.

"OK. Well… first of all, thank you for trusting me. Do you want to tell your dad?"

"No. Not yet."

"OK." I think, fast. I do not want to be responsible for keeping this huge thing from Sam. But I do want Sophie to know she can trust me. I suppose, until we have something definite to tell him, it's OK to keep quiet.

"So what's the situation? Your period's late, is that it?" It's a stupid question, I know, with an obvious answer. She nods.

"How late?"

"I haven't had one since late June."

Shit.

"But I am quite irregular. It has been this long between them, before."

"OK," I say. "That's interesting. And you've been… careful… so it could just be your body playing tricks on you."

"Yes, but I think I feel different. I'm sure I do." She is tearful again.

"Alright, well, I think we know what we have to do."

"A test?" she asks.

"Yes. A test. I'll get one. You can do it at home, when your dad's at work… is that OK?'

I do feel uncomfortable, withholding this from Sam. But it's only for a day at most, I reason.

"Alright, we'll get one on the way back home," I say. "Let's walk for a bit, and then head back through town. I'll tuck the test away somewhere, and I'll come back at lunchtime tomorrow, and you can do it then. OK?"

"OK. Thank you, Alice."

"It's alright," I say. "It's quite alright."

We walk along the beach, and arrive at the rocks where the two of us first met, when Sophie was nine. Half the age she is now. But eighteen is not a very big age to be half of. I remember seeing Kate all glamorous and pristine, on her phone, a little way off. And she had seemed young, to have a nine-year-old daughter. I suppose she was. But she was a few years older than Sophie is now, when she was pregnant. How odd it is, that she and Sam were together. I can't see it now. But they'd have made a beautiful couple. Had beautiful children, if they'd stayed together. As it is, they have Sophie, and she might not be Sam's biological daughter, but she is very definitely his.

We turn and walk back towards the town, clipping Meg's lead on to walk along the path above the rocks, and round up to the harbour. There is only one chemist shop in town, but they are very discreet. Nevertheless, I feel my palms sweating as we approach. "You hold Meg," I say to Sophie. "I'll just be a minute."

I put on my face mask, and push open the door, the bell ringing. It's that kind of old-fashioned shop, and the tourists love it.

"Alice!" I hear, and I am grateful for my mask, to hide the fact that my face must have dropped at the sight of her. What am I going to do now?

Karen is waiting for Ron's prescription and it's taking 'ages' she says, with a sigh. I can't very well pretend I'm there for a prescription, as I don't have one to hand, and besides, I'd then have to make up an illness, for me or for Sam, or one of the kids, and she'd ask Sam, and it would spiral out of control. At the same time, I can't go rooting round for a pregnancy test.

"Did you have a good weekend away?" she asks.

"It was lovely, thank you."

"Nice and restful?"

"Oh yes, yes thank you."

"Are you alright?" she asks, eyeing me suspiciously.

"I'm fine, thanks." She doesn't say anything, but looks at me expectantly. "Oh, you mean, because I'm…?"

Still, she just looks at me. I can feel my face getting red.

"I just need some toothpaste," I finish with.

"Alright," she says, and I know now she doesn't believe me.

"Actually," I say, desperate to cut short any suspicion she might have that another grandchild might be on its way, "it's not toothpaste. It's a bit embarrassing, but since I had covid, I've had a bit of an… an upset stomach."

"Oh, have you, love? I'm sorry, I didn't know."

"No, well, you wouldn't. I haven't really told anyone. Not even Sam," I say.

"It's nothing to be ashamed of, Alice," she says, but I now can see that she is feeling quite pleased that I've confided in her, just as I felt when Sophie told me her news.

"I know, I know… it's just not very nice, you know?"

"Oh I know. Well, you'd better get yourself something, and get home, just in case…"

"Yes, you're right. I'd better."

So I go to the counter, and ask for something to stop diarrhoea. And then I have to answer twenty questions about it, and leave with a promise to tell my GP if it doesn't clear up soon. Karen shoots me a sympathetic look and I leave the shop.

"Did you get it?" Sophie asks, eagerly.

"No," I say, and I relay the story of bumping into Karen, which makes her laugh.

"I'm glad you find it funny," I say, and really, I am. It's nice to see her smile.

In the end, I take an extended lunch break the next day, and we go to the supermarket out of town, where we get a box of three tests. We go into the toilets there, and Sophie does the test in one of the cubicles. Not the most lovely place to find out if you're going to be a mother, but needs must. I go into the cubicle, after she's done what she needs to do, and we lock ourselves in. She is shaking.

"Whatever happens, Soph, it will be OK," I say.

"I know," she says in a small voice, and she looks so young.

"We all love you. You've got such great parents, and step-parents. And we'll do everything we can to make things OK."

"I've been such an idiot!" she says.

"You have not," I respond firmly. "You have been a perfectly normal teenager, and you've been sensible, anyway. But even if you hadn't, Soph, things happen. Besides," I can't help myself, "this is partly Rory's doing, as well!"

"I know. It is. I feel bad I haven't told him. But I just don't know what I'd do if I'm… I want to know first, and make a decision before I tell him."

I find myself feeling a bit sorry for Rory; if Sophie is pregnant, it does affect him hugely, yet he has no idea. And he is unlikely to have much of a say in the matter, because it's her body, and it would be her being pregnant, and giving birth, and having a child for the rest of her life. It would be Rory's child, too, of course, but he'd no doubt find it easier to cut ties, if that's the kind of person he is – and I'm not saying he is. I don't know. But it has to be her decision.

These thoughts run through my head, like a reel of film. I see Sophie in the different stages of pregnancy; in the labour room; with a newborn; stuck at home, frazzled, while her friends are off to uni and out clubbing.

I see Sam and me looking after her baby while she goes off to college.

I see the pregnancy test stick.

I see she is not pregnant.

I point at it, and she follows my gaze. She is terrified, and it takes her a moment to register the sight, and then she is relieved, and then she is crying, and we're hugging, and she disposes of the pregnancy test in the sanitary towel bin, and I pull the flush, although I don't know why, and we leave the cubicle together, to the surprise of the grey-haired lady who is just coming into the toilets.

Back at home, Sam has put Holly and Ben to bed, and I hug him, and kiss him. "Let's open some wine," I say. "Sophie, want a glass?" I ask, as she walks into the kitchen.

"Yes, please," she says, and she smiles widely. We had a good talk on the way back home, and we decided to keep this between ourselves, except that she is going to tell Rory what happened.

"What do you think he'd have said, if you were pregnant?"

"I don't know," she admitted. "I think… I think he might have been pleased."

"Really?"

"Well, yeah, maybe. I can imagine he'd like the idea of being a dad."

"I know what you mean. It's easy to like the idea of something. It's bloody hard work, being a parent, though.

I'm glad I was a bit older when I had Ben. I got to enjoy life a lot first."

"Mum was young when she had me."

"Yes, she was. And I think she loved it. And the thing is, life happens. Not always as you expect, or as you plan, but look at your mum now. She's got you, and she's got Jacob, and Isaac, and a brilliant business, in a beautiful place. I don't think she would change a thing. Still," I add, "maybe better to try not to get pregnant just yet."

"Don't worry," she said. "I am going to make sure I don't."

"Are you alright?" Sam asks, uncorking the wine while Sophie goes to put her phone on charge. She's actually putting the box of pregnancy tests away, before Sam sees them. We should maybe have just binned them, because I also am not planning on getting pregnant, but it seemed a bit wasteful; and maybe they'll come in handy for somebody else sometime.

"I'm fine thanks, why?" I ask, almost defensively. Maybe he has picked up that there was something going on.

"Oh, Mum rang. Said she saw you in the chemist's, and you've got a bad stomach."

Karen, I curse inwardly. I should have known she couldn't keep her mouth shut.

"Yes, it's something and nothing, really," I say. "It's quite common, post-covid, I think."

"Bloody covid," he says, pulling me to him and kissing the top of my head. "You should have said, though. I'd have gone to the chemist for you."

"Oh, it's fine. Like I said, something and nothing."

Thank god she didn't see me getting pregnancy tests.

32

Soon enough, the town is snuggling down into autumn. I like to walk out with Meg in the early evening, up the coastal path a little way, and look back at the beautiful place where we live. At this time of day just a few short weeks ago, the beaches would have still been populated with holiday-makers and their colourful paraphernalia. Now, there is a wide-open space down there, with a handful of other walkers also trying to make the most of the last vestiges of daylight. Beyond the beach, the buildings stack up, along the slopes to the top of town. Many already have lights on; some have curtains closed, with just the tiniest sliver of light pressing through the edges. It's a cosy scene, and reminds me that even though summer has passed for another year, there is still much to be enjoyed.

Already, Ben has been at school for a month. We crossed that first-day hurdle with relative ease. OK, I may have shed a tear or two, but he had happily walked into his new classroom, guided in by a smiling teaching assistant. The classroom door shutting marked a new stage of life, where my little boy is just less little, and will increase in independence every year. A good thing. A great thing. But I still mourn those unforgettable baby and toddler days.

Sarah, who I first met at the church baby group when Ben was a baby, was dropping off the twins at the same time, and smiling widely. Becky, who had Zach just days before Ben was born, was in a flood of tears.

"Coffee?" I asked. "I have to get to work, but I am sure that today of all days I can get away with being half an hour late."

"Same," said Sarah. "It does help if you're your own boss."

So the three of us walked down to Joe's, and treated ourselves to not only coffee, but crumpets as well. And we toasted each other for having got our boys to this stage of life.

"I was sure I'd have killed at least one of the twins by now," Sarah said. "But no, both still going strong."

Becky, apparently over the worst, smiled. "I felt the same. My god, I loved having a baby, but I was terrified, too. The responsibility!"

"Don't remind me," I said. "I remember the first time I drove Ben to the supermarket, just me and him. I was terrified I'd crash, or that somebody would drive into the side where his seat was. It's bloody nerve-racking. Poor old Holly doesn't receive anywhere near as much attention. She just has to crack on with things."

"It'll be good for her in the long run," said Sarah.

"And now I'm starting all over again." Becky was smiling almost shyly, her hand on her tummy.

"Oh my god! I had no idea. Congratulations, Becky," I said, reaching across to hug her.

"Thanks. But just tell me two is good, OK?"

"Oh yeah, two's great!" said Sarah.

"Two is perfect," I added.

"I'm not sure if you're being sarcastic!" Becky grinned. "But I'm happy. And Andy's over the moon. I know he's hoping for a girl. I really don't mind, either way."

"Exactly… what does it matter?"

I think again of Sophie, and am grateful for that near-miss. She actually, typically, went on to get her period the very next day. Perhaps a coincidence, or perhaps the fact that she was no longer as stressed as she had been. Either way, it doesn't really matter. What is important is that she is OK, and she's back in Devon again now, working at the local supermarket, and saving money to go away for the second half of her gap year. Rory is back at uni, and as far as I know, they are very much still 'on', although I don't know if she told him about the pregnancy scare. For my part, I haven't mentioned it to Sam, or to Kate, or to anyone. Not even Julie. Sophie trusted me, and I am so very pleased that she did. I reason that if Sophie had been pregnant, then of course I'd have told them. It would have been pretty hard to keep that a secret for long anyway! But as it is, there was nothing to it. If Sophie wants to tell them, she can, but I suspect that for her it is already old history. Life moves on.

Since starting school, Ben has been to two birthday parties for classmates, where every child in the class has been invited, so I am beginning to recognise some of the other parents. It really helps, already knowing Sarah and Becky so well, though. I have a ready-made little nest of vipers, as Julie calls us. "You're just jealous," I say. "It'll be your turn soon enough. You can create your own nest."

I can tell Ben's getting tired from all the long days, and from having to be well-behaved all the time. It's a good job half-term is just weeks away. I make extra sure I spend time with him in the evenings, and we normally work on his reading together. But tonight it's a town council meeting, and I have promised Bea that I will go with her. She's keen to become re-involved with things locally, and I suspect she is just trying to fill as much of her time as she can. Dad was meant to be coming, too, but Mum's coming in his place, as he's worn out. He's still having headaches, and doesn't have much of an appetite. The only explanation anyone can come up with is long covid. How I look forward to the day we never have to hear that particular c-word again!

The room is full for the meeting, taking me back to that business network earlier in the year, when I first met Crazy Craig. I don't really feel like his nickname does him justice, to be honest. It's like he's trying to portray himself as this larger-than-life character, when he is actually as sensitive and vulnerable as the rest of us. I have seen him a few times around town over the summer, and in fact one of those parties Ben went to had a couple of his bouncy castles, though I didn't see Craig himself that day. I hope it means things are looking up for him. I scan the room for him now, but I can't see any sign of him.

There is Diane, though, sitting neatly at the front. She must get to these things an hour early; she's always in one of the best seats. Mum, Bea and I squeeze our way into three seats together, in the penultimate row from the back. The general chatter dies down as Peter Oswald, the mayor, takes the stage.

"Good evening, everyone," he says, to a muttered response, and then an "Evening, Pete!" from somebody at the back, which draws a few laughs.

"Ron," Peter smiles and nods, and I turn to see that it is

indeed Ron, my stepfather-in-law, grinning good-naturedly.

"I trust you're all well and enjoyed the summer. How is your place now, Diane?" he addresses her directly. I can't hear her answer very well, but presumably it is positive, as Peter smiles and nods. "Smashing. And I know the pizza shop's back on its feet, and the residential and holiday properties are almost all refurbished as well. This is what's great about a community like ours. We all pull together, and look out for one another.

"Now, it was a great shame that we had to cancel the festival, but next year is shaping up for something even bigger and better, with the jubilee in June. It has been proposed, by Phil Griffiths at the Sail Loft, that we reinstate this year's failed festival, as part of the bigger jubilee celebrations. He can't be here tonight, but I know he's offered to be on the planning committee and has put his name forward for chair, if that is to everyone's liking." I look at Mum, to see she's smiling. I don't know how Dad's going to find the energy to work on the planning committee as well as at the hotel. But I feel proud to hear his name mentioned, and received so well. It really does feel like we're part of the town now – Cornish or not, we've found our place. "What I'd suggest is that we take a vote tonight, to decide if we would like to try again with the festival, and if everyone is happy for it to be a part of the larger celebrations. After all, the original idea was to have a festival for the people of the town, more than for our very welcome visitors." There is a little smatter of applause at this. "If we work it into the jubilee celebrations, during the extended bank holiday weekend, I think we will have to accept we will be swamped with tourists, too."

"But if we don't do it then, when will we?" Diane says, standing up. She may be short, but she knows how to project her voice when she wants to. "I say we do it. God knows, we need some highlights to look forward to, and I for one don't mind sharing them with the emmets... I mean, holidaymakers." This gets a laugh, as well, and Diane looks pleased. I haven't seen this side of her before.

"All in favour, raise your hands," Peter says, and almost everyone, if not everyone, in the room, puts a hand in the air.

"Will we be able to get the fair that weekend, though?" somebody asks. I can't see who it is.

"I've already asked," Peter says, "and disappointingly, no."

Diane, still standing, speaks up again. "I know a gentleman who would be more than happy to provide his bouncy castles, which could go on the rugby field instead of the fair. I've already mentioned it to Peter. I know it's not the same as a fairground—"

"Might not be as many fights!" another voice shouts.

"This the bloke that got washed out to sea?" someone else asks.

I notice Diane's face flush a little, but whether it is anger on Craig's behalf, or something else, I can't tell. "Yes, it's Craig Cash. He's keen to do something for the town as a whole, and I know he isn't intending to charge anything for the bouncy castle hire. I think it's his way of thanking us." She sits abruptly down, perhaps trying to avoid any more attention.

"I think it's very generous of him," says Peter. "And it's one for the committee, I think. So, if anyone here would like to get involved in planning the celebrations next June, please contact Phil Griffiths at the Sail Loft Hotel. Or his wife, Sue, is here tonight. Can you put your hand up please, Sue?"

Mum, red-faced, stands and puts her hand up. A few people turn and smile at her, and she sits down again, looking relieved to do so.

"So, next on the agenda. The drainage system." The topics change fast, as Peter is an expert at this. Unfortunately, he is standing down at the end of the year, and I know a few of the contenders who are next in line won't be quite as professional as him. But all of these people are so entwined with the town, and perhaps they do want the accolade of being a mayor, or a local councillor, but at the same time, they are putting their energy and their time into something for the benefit of all. Who knows, maybe Dad will be throwing his hat in the ring one day. Councillor Philip Griffiths. Scrub that – Mayor Philip Griffiths. It sounds pretty good.

About twenty minutes into the meeting, I hear the door open for some latecomers, and I notice more than one head turns round, then does a double-take. I have to have a look myself, and I turn to see Lydia, with none other than Si Davey. To his credit, he looks a bit self-conscious. What on earth is he doing at the town council meeting?

"Thank you for joining us, Lydia and Simon." Peter smiles. "I know you've had to rush to get here, but I think everyone here will be happy to hear the news that Simon has agreed to do our Christmas lights switch-on this year." There is an audible group gasp at the news. "I know it is normally my honour, as mayor, but I didn't think any of you would mind too much, if I stepped aside for this young man."

I see Si is actually red-faced, too. Who'd have thought he had such humility? But I suppose, just like anyone, in a room full of people he doesn't know, having such attention turned on him is not wholly comfortable.

"Thank you, Peter," he manages. I notice Paul Waters and Shona are close by, and Paul reaches across to give Si a congratulatory squeeze of the arm. Typical Paul, not to be in the least bit starstruck, but Si smiles gratefully.

Well, that last bit of news has everyone talking, and it's very hard to get a focus on the remaining agenda items, but Peter battles heroically through, and we eventually reach the end. Si, to his credit, stays through all of this, and I can imagine him thinking some of the characters in the room might be good inspiration for future acting roles. We certainly have our share of interesting personalities.

Eventually, Peter draws the meeting to a close, and we all file out, into the still night air. It's not all that cold, and I am reluctant to go straight home. I will have missed Ben and Holly's bedtimes, anyway.

"Fancy a drink?" I suggest to Mum and Bea.

"I was just going to say the same thing!" Bea laughs.

"Alice!" I feel a hand on my arm, and turn to see Lydia, whose other hand, I can't fail to notice, is snug in Si Davey's.

"Hello," I say, hugging her, and smiling at Si. "We're just going for a drink. Care to join us?" I hope Mum and Bea don't mind.

"That would be lovely," Lydia says, looking to Si, who smiles and gives a nod.

The five of us walk down to the Mainbrace, and we find a table tucked away at the back. Even so, Si's presence doesn't go unnoticed, and there are a few taps on shoulders, and nods towards our table.

"That must be annoying!" I say.

"It's OK. No, you're right, it is a bit annoying," Si admits. "But it comes with the territory."

"I have a feeling that if you're here a bit, though, you'll soon become less of a novelty. It's that kind of place, really. Most people are pretty down to earth, and you'll become part of the furniture." I hope I'm not saying too much. But I suspect that for him to be agreeing to the Christmas lights switch-on, and to have appeared with Lydia at the town meeting, things are fairly steady between them.

I can see Lydia smiling. "I think Simon will be here fairly often," she says.

Simon! I love it. Somehow, lengthening his name rather than shortening it, suggests intimacy. He smiles at her, in such a way that suggests he'd be more than happy to never leave.

"We'll protect you from the tourists, too, if you become one of us," Bea laughs. It's good to see her smiling.

I feel like we're trespassing a little too far into Si and Lydia's personal space now, so I change the subject. "Anyway, Mum, how on earth is Dad going to manage all this committee stuff, and the Sail Loft? He's already worn out."

"Ah, yes, well, Bea and your dad and I have been chatting, and we've got a plan."

"Oh yes?"

"Yes. Bea is coming back to the Sail Loft!"

"You're selling up?"

"No, we're keeping it. But Bea's going to join us, as the

manager. Like you were, for her. And I'm taking over the kitchen duties. Your dad's going to teach me. He needs a break, Alice. And to be honest, I've had enough of computers, and phones, and all that. Your dad and I'll be working with Bea, but she'll be running the hotel day-to-day."

"Bloody hell, life in this place is like a roundabout! I can't keep up."

"But it works, doesn't it, Alice? Your dad needs a break, your mum needs a change, and I need to be busy," says Bea. "And I need familiarity."

"Won't you feel weird, though, working there for somebody else?"

"I don't know," she admits. "But time will tell."

"Well, great," I say. "It is a special place to work."

"It is," agrees Lydia.

"To the Sail Loft," I say, raising my glass. Around the table, there are four of us who have either worked at, lived in, and/or owned the Sail Loft Hotel over the years.

The fifth person, Si Davey, gamely raises his glass as well.

It's closing time when we leave, and the assorted remaining drinkers jangle out of the pub, as though it's emptying out its pockets onto the pavement. We leave last, so as to shield Si as best we can. Even in the space of a couple of hours, he has become familiar, and more, well, normal, so that I no longer feel the need to grin like an imbecile at him, to show him how unfazed I am by his presence.

He and Lydia hug us all goodbye. *I've just been hugged by Si Davey!* I think. So perhaps I'm not entirely over his celebrity yet.

Mum and Bea chat away as we walk up the hill, and I lag slightly behind. I do love the summer, but I had forgotten how much I appreciate the quiet of autumn, and peace of winter. The streets now are empty enough to allow our footsteps to reverberate from the walls, and I can hear the sea some way behind us, below the town.

This time last year, we were headed for a sharp, cold winter, and another lockdown; an excruciatingly lonely and stressful time for many. *Please don't let us have the same again*, I beg of an unknown entity. Imagine if Ben, just having started school, is pulled out, to have to learn at home. How would we manage that? And how would it affect him? Last year's reception classes had just that. But maybe they're too young for it to have a real impact. Too little to appreciate how scary covid is, and the way it's ravaged the country. The world, in fact. For many of us, there has been minimal impact; on the surface, at least. But, like a tidal wave, it has engulfed us all, taking victim after victim, with no compassion. Loved ones have been left like seaweed, stranded and limp on the shore. Only in its retreat will its full effects be revealed, and even if on the surface all looks much the same, even the smoothest section of sand will have shifted slightly.

Time to try again!

Our wonderful town is looking beautiful, decked out once more with colourful bunting, and fresh, cheerful hanging baskets outside shop doorways. There are posters on every wall, every lamp-post, in houses, shops, pubs, cafes… drumming up excitement for the upcoming Jubilee celebrations; almost exactly a year since the Festival That Never Happened.

It is testament to the town that there is no evidence of the flood which caused last year's event to be cancelled. All affected buildings were emptied and dried out within weeks, with renovations beginning soon after. Diane Norris, of the Cut & Di Salon, says that she could not have managed without the support of local residents and other businesses. Vinyl Ritchie Records allowed her to utilise their attic space as a makeshift salon, while her own premises were put back in order. Meanwhile, the Dough Nuts pizza company was able to keep producing their popular takeaway pizzas thanks to the kindness of a handful of B&Bs, who allowed Caleb Rossi and his team to utilise their kitchens.

"They set up a rota," says Caleb, "and we were able to make and deliver pizzas to order, as long as we cleared up every evening so that the important breakfast element of the B&Bs could still go ahead. I am so grateful to all the wonderful people who helped to make this happen."

As a reaction to the vulnerability of the Dough Nuts premises, Caleb and partner Maria have purchased a mobile pizza unit, and plan to service weddings, country fayres and festivals, and other events. "It was not ideal, but the flood was a bit of a wake-up call. The lockdowns, too," says Maria. "We had to think and move fast, to keep our business running." The Dough Nuts van will be on the rugby field on Festival Day, so make sure you pop over to see them.

While last year's planned event was aimed primarily at the local population, this year's is a double, make that triple, celebration.

Local councillor Phil Griffiths has this to say: "It's like a collective sigh of relief – that we might just be able to put covid behind us, or at the very least live with it, and that this year has been lockdown-free. At the same time, we are celebrating the Platinum Jubilee, and with the extra bank holiday, the town is likely to be very busy. Precautions have been put in place to ensure everyone is safe and free to enjoy our special event."

With festivities set to last the full four days of the weekend, beginning with the lighting of the beacon on the Island on Thursday evening, there is much to look forward to. We will just have to keep our fingers crossed that the weather is kind to us this year.

Epilogue

It is with a rush of relief and joy that I open the curtains to the bluest of skies, and a sun already high in the sky. In fact, the weather has been wonderful almost all week, and despite fears caused by last year's disastrous events, we have sailed through the last few days. It is half-term, so it has been busy. Amethi is fully booked, but all the guests have been extremely low-maintenance.

They are all families with school-age children, and keen to get out and about, and make the most of the long, light evenings. Julie has provided picnics and packed lunches, and the occasional evening meal, but, really, I think these people are just enjoying having time to themselves. They don't even want the bother of having to interact with somebody who has cooked them dinner; they'd rather just stay self-contained.

The spectre of covid is still very much present, and the Robinson family said they were worried they'd have to cancel their holiday as Mrs Robinson tested positive the week before they were due here. "I was quite ill with it, but I seem to have bounced back. I am sure being at Amethi has helped. And Lizzie's yoga and meditation sessions."

"Yes, Lizzie's very good at seeing what people need," I said. "Hopefully she's taken it easy with you."

"Oh, so easy," Mrs Robinson laughed, and rolled her

shoulders back. I could almost feel her muscles relaxing and knots loosening.

So all is well up at Amethi, and Lizzie, being neither a royalist nor very keen on crowds, has happily agreed to stay on site and be on hand for the new arrivals on Saturday. She's even going to have Meg overnight, as this year Dad – being a newly elected local councillor – is going to be very much involved in the goings-on in town. He says it was really quite simple to arrange the Saturday celebrations, as they already had a blueprint from last year. There are just a few tweaks, to make the event fit the jubilee as well, including the addition of a big screen down at the harbour, onto which the jubilee celebrations in London can be projected. The concert band will be playing at the harbourside too, and the town's newly-formed answer to the Fisherman's Friends will be singing there, as will the primary school choir. Mum is not quite as excited as Dad by the whole thing, and says she'll pop down for an hour or two, but otherwise she'll be at the Sail Loft if anyone needs her.

Much like last year, the plan is for Sam, me, Holly and Ben to meet up with Julie, Luke and Zinnia, and to head down to town together. We are missing Sophie, who is currently in Spain with Janie and Jon. Her old friend Amber is out there, too, and it sounds like they're having the time of their lives.

Poor Rory is a thing of the past – dumped unceremoniously by Sophie at New Year ("Just as I was starting to like him," Sam had said, but I know he was pleased really). To Sophie, it was time to move on.

"I didn't want to be tied down, when I'm about to go

travelling round Europe," she explained, in quite a red-faced way, when Sam asked her what had happened.

In private, she told me that the pregnancy scare had really got her thinking, about Rory, and relationships in general.

"I thought, if I couldn't handle being pregnant, then maybe I'm not mature enough to be sleeping with anyone at all. And the more I imagined being a parent, with Rory as the father, the less I could see myself with him."

I think this last point is the more pertinent one. I am sure she might very well change her mind on the sex front, the next time she meets somebody she has a connection with. But the possibility of being pregnant really did shock her, and make her consider things more closely. It still crosses my mind, sometimes, how different things could have been, if it had been more than a scare. But there is no point wasting too much time worrying about something that never was.

Zinnia is perched high on Luke's shoulders, and as we reach them, she pats Sam on the head and giggles.

"Who did that?" Sam says, looking around him, much to Zinnia's delight.

"Up, Daddy! Up!" Holly says, wanting to be the same as her girl-idol. Ben, meanwhile, a grown-up schoolboy, stays firmly grounded, tugging at my hand and eager to get down to the town.

"Alright, alright!" I laugh, and Julie comes round to take his other hand, so we can swing him on the way down. He belly-laughs as his little legs swoosh into the air.

The further down the hill we go, the busier the pavements become; there are trickles of people coming down the various side streets, and combining to create a wider flow; a nice comparison to last year's rainwater, which rushed down these same streets, gathering strength as its volume increased on the approach to town.

I hold Ben's hand more tightly, and glance back to make sure Holly is still safe on Sam's shoulders. I needn't have worried. She and Zinnia are holding hands, looking down on the rest of us, and happy as can be.

As we ease our way in amongst the crowds, we head purposefully towards the harbour, knowing that there should be more space there. And as luck would have it, a table comes free outside the Mainbrace, and Luke scoots in, his daughter still attached to his shoulders.

"Shotgun!" he calls.

"I'm not sure that's quite right, Luke," says Julie, but we gratefully join him. I try not to look around to see whose toes we might have trampled on.

"Good work, mate," says Sam.

"Comes from all my years in London, doesn't it?" grins Luke. "It's a dog-cat-dog world, ain't it?"

"Dogs eat dogs?" Ben asks, puzzled and slightly perturbed by this idea.

"Just a saying, Benny," Luke laughs. "It means sometimes you've got to go for what you want, or somebody else will just take it anyway."

Ben considers this idea.

"Let's go and get some drinks," I say to Julie.

"Good idea."

We patiently join the queue for the bar, and I notice that even now we are approaching our forties, Julie never fails to catch people's attention. She's tall, and slim and striking, with her dark skin and black hair; they make her stand out, but no less than her smile and her general air of confidence and positivity. She is rarely fazed by anything, and never afraid to ask for what she wants. She takes my hand now, and somehow manages to squeeze us through a couple of rows of people, without anyone saying a word.

"You and Luke make a perfect pair," I laugh.

"Dog-eat-dog, like he said."

And a little part of me feels justified, here amongst the throngs of holiday-makers who are crowding out the pub. This is our town, I think. We have a place here. I have a quiet word with myself. I'll be calling them emmets next. Anyway, there is no animosity, and everyone seems happy enough to wait to be served. There are hours of entertainment and fun ahead, and the sun is shining. It's a good day, I think, and I realise I'm smiling.

"What are you grinning about?" asks Julie.

"Oh, nothing," I say, leaning close to her so she can hear me. "Well – nothing, and everything. Remember when we came in here, that night just after we got back to Cornwall?"

"Oh yeah… the night we saw Luke again!"

"And when I saw Sam…"

"From a distance."

"Yes," I acknowledge, remembering the shock of recognising his silhouette in front of the fire. "So funny to think of all that's happened since then."

A gap comes free at the bar, and Julie seizes the opportunity. She orders two pints each for the adults, cartons of apple juice for the children, and various bags of crisps. She even somehow manages to convince a nearby bloke to help carry all the glasses out to the table. His face falls slightly when he sees Luke sitting there.

"Thanks so much!" Julie says airily, sending him on his way once he's deposited the drinks, and setting down three pints herself. I put down the two I'm carrying, and pluck the apple juices out of my pockets.

"You are a bloody nightmare!" Luke laughs to his wife. "That poor bloke!"

"What? He was just being helpful. Very much in the spirit of the day." She almost looks innocent, sliding into the seat next to him.

"Sure," he says, and kisses her on the lips, and they look at each other for a moment, smiling.

"Alright, you two! Get a room!" Sam says.

"Get a room?" Ben puzzles.

"Oh, yeah, like, make some room," Sam responds quickly. "Look, Lydia and Si are here, we'd better budge up."

I stand and wave to Lydia, and she smiles, turning to say something to Si. They head over to us.

"Best seats in the house!" Lydia says. "How did you manage this?"

"It's all thanks to Luke," says Julie.

"Hi, Si," I say. "You OK?"

"Yes, thanks, Alice. A bit tired, but it's good to be back." He's been abroad, filming in Italy. "Can I get anyone a drink?"

"We're all OK thanks," I say. "Are you sure you'll be alright in amongst all that lot, though?" I gesture to the crowds of people inside and outside the pub.

"I have my trusty cap, thanks, Alice." He pulls a baseball cap from his pocket and firmly down on his head. "See, I'm like Batman. Nobody will know my real identity."

"Pratman, more like," Lydia says, and they grin at each

other. Looks like Julie and Luke are not the only ones in need of a room.

As Si begins the journey towards the bar, I hear somebody say, "He looks like that bloke off the telly."

We keep our table all afternoon and into the evening. It's the perfect place to sit and watch the goings-on. David, Martin and Bea find us, and perch on the wall while we make space for Tyler and Esme.

When the children begin to get bored, Julie, David and I take them for a walk, leaving the others to guard our table. We wander along through the crowds, but it's hard work with the children, and we find ourselves joining a bus queue. Before long, we are being jiggled along on the bumpy seats around the tight, steep streets and up towards the rugby club. We disembark there, and head into the field, where to the children's great delight we are greeted by the sight of numerous bright bouncy castles.

They dash towards the nearest one, discarding their shoes for us to pick up. Tyler and Esme help Holly up, and my heart is in my mouth as I watch her get bounced into the air by the weight of some of the bigger kids, but she seems to be in her element, and more than able to hold her own.

"This is much better than a fair," I say to Julie, looking around the field. "I don't think I can stomach fairground rides anymore – I'm too old."

"Not as many fights on bouncy castles, either," she says.

When our red-faced children eventually scramble down, we help them get their shoes back on, and go in search of a drink. I see Craig near the Dough Nuts van, and I go to say hello.

"Hi, Alice," he says, and kisses me on the cheek. He is grinning from ear to ear.

"Hi, Craig," I say, touched by the warmth of his greeting. "This is great!"

"It's alright, isn't it?"

"I'll say! You've done a brilliant job. The kids love it."

"Not just the kids," says David. "Can you watch my two, and hold my shoes, for a minute?" He doesn't wait for an answer, but whips off his trainers and hands them to me, then makes a beeline for one of the giant inflatable slides. I shake my head in mock-disappointment as he bumps his way down, laughing with glee.

"One more time?" he calls over.

"Go on then!"

David scampers off again, and I have a vision of what he must have been like as a child.

"So, how's your year been, Craig?" I venture, wondering if it's not really my place to be asking such a question.

"I won't lie, it's been tough," he says. "Winter, especially. And in March, I really was on the verge of leaving. My first year was almost up, and I suppose I'd already decided it wasn't going to work. I almost wanted to go back up home, and wallow in my misery. I suppose I felt like I deserved it."

I don't know what to say to this, so just let him talk.

"But something changed, about the time the clocks did," he continues, "and the weather got nicer, and the days got longer, and, well, actually, here's another reason…"

He extends his arm towards none other than Diane Norris, the hairdresser. She smilingly accepts his invitation, and moves in towards him, her petite form looking even smaller next to Craig's bulk. She puts her arms around him, but they barely reach around his middle.

"Hi Diane," I say.

"Hello, Alice. Isn't this wonderful?" Her face is flushed, and she looks radiant.

"It really is," I say. "And you look very happy."

"I am. We are! Aren't we?" She looks up at Craig.

"We are," he confirms.

"Who'd have thought this time last year, what we'd be doing now?" says Diane.

"Indeed," Craig kisses the top of her head.

"Well, I'm really pleased for you both. And Craig, you know you're going to have to make this an annual thing?"

"I'd be happy to, Alice," he semi-bows.

David comes bowling over to pluck his shoes from my hands. "Let's get pizza!" he says.

I roll my eyes at Craig and Diane. "He's supposed to be one of the responsible adults!" I laugh. "We'd better go, though, Julie's got all five kids over there." I can just make out my friend on the ground, her hair being decorated with daisies by the children. "I think she might need rescuing."

David takes orders for pizzas, while I sit down with Julie and the children. It's nice to sit on the outskirts and watch the goings-on.

"Are they an item now, then?" Julie asks, looking at Craig and Diane, who are holding hands. From behind, they almost look like father and daughter.

"Looks like it," I say.

"That's pretty lovely."

"Seems like this is the perfect place to fall in love," I say.

Tyler makes a pretend-sick noise. "I'm never being in love," he says.

"No?"

"No. I'm going to live with my friends, and I'm definitely not having kids."

"What's wrong with kids?" I ask.

"They're… we're…"

I get the feeling he hasn't really thought this through.

"Nothing," he begrudges. "But I don't want to be a dad."

"Well, you might change your mind one day. Or you might not. Either way is fine. But you've certainly got some good examples of dads to follow."

I smile at David, who is coming toward us, a pile of pizza boxes in his arms, secured in place by his chin. He unloads them onto the grass, and we all tuck in. There is definitely something to be said for eating outside, under the summer sun.

We make our way back down to town on the bus, and return to the Mainbrace. The children are tired by now, but they sit happily with some colouring-in that Julie seems to have produced from somewhere, while we adults chat and half-watch the celebrations in London.

"I'd rather be in Cornwall," I say.

"Always," says Sam.

As the daylight dims, and the harbour is illuminated with twinkling lights, I scan the happy faces of the crowd, and then the shops and restaurants along the harbour front. I feel a rush of love for this place; for this day; for the people I am with. Sitting by Bea, I squeeze her arm lightly. "Are you OK?"

"As OK as I could be, I think. Thank you, Alice. I'm in the right place, at least. With the right people, to help me through."

"I'm glad. I can't imagine, Bea, really."

"You don't have to. The best thing you can do, for yourself and for me, is just enjoy what you've got. Your family. Your husband."

I glance across at Sam and catch his eye. He smiles.

"I do, enjoy them," I say. "And appreciate them. I mean, not all the time. Sometimes they're really bloody annoying!" Bea laughs at this, I'm glad to see. "But I do appreciate them."

"I know you do. And you know some people say you should live every day like it's your last... well, you can't. You just can't. Life's not like that. It's busy and hectic, and some days you just want to go to bed and wake up the following morning. And god knows, Bob used to drive me mad sometimes! He'd never put anything in the dishwasher, just *near* the dishwasher. And he had a huge pile of dirty clothes on the floor on his side of the bed! Living with someone is hard work. It's a compromise. And maybe it was all the more so for me, because I'd been on my own for so long before I met him. But he was good, and kind, and funny, and just so loving. I miss him every day."

I feel a lump in my throat, listening to her, and I know that my eyes will be shining in the light.

"But I'd always rather have had him, for those few short years, and endure this... this pain–" she thumps her chest – "than to never have had him at all. But being with you and Sam, and David and Martin, Julie and Luke – even Lydia and her gorgeous actor! – it makes me feel happy. It's what life is all about. I don't mean work isn't important. You and I both know it is, especially for us women. We've worked too hard to belittle our achievements. But when all's said and done, it's the people that matter."

We are quiet for a few moments, watching the concert band setting up along the harbour wall, the boats rocking softly before them. The night sky is almost violet in the soft twilight, and the evening air feels magical to me.

All around me are groups of family and friends, who for a large part of the last year or two will have been unable to see each other. Unable to go to the pub, or the café, for a drink and a chat – for a while not even allowed to sit on a park bench together, or go for a walk. Dad's quote in that article, about today being a collective sigh of relief, is just right. We are the lucky ones. We have survived. After all the sadness and stress and anxiety, maybe it's OK to celebrate, even if it's just for one day.

David, returning from the toilet, squeezes in next to Bea and puts his arm around her. She leans against him.

A slight breeze ruffles the bunting and makes the lights dance up and down. Across from me, my husband and son are engaged in a game of rock, paper, scissors, and almost beside themselves with laughter.

My daughter clambers across the table, navigating the glasses and half-empty chip cartons with ease. She climbs onto my lap, putting her face against my neck, and wrapping the soft material of my hoodie around her fingers. I push my face into her hair and breathe in. She smells of banana shampoo, and pizza; salty sea air, and childhood. I close my eyes, and focus on her warmth and her small weight, listening to the voices all around me, and then the hush that descends as the band starts up, their first notes floating high up into the air, and drifting away, across the waves.

Acknowledgements

I will start with the thank yous – as usual, there are quite a few! Beginning this time with Catherine Clarke, whose name some of you must be familiar with by now! Catherine is the talented artist and designer I have to thank for all my beautiful book covers, and many of the other Heddon Publishing covers, too. She is not only brilliant at her work but she is a valued friend, and loads of fun, and I can only think that we were destined to meet. You can (and should!) see more of her work at:
www.catherineclarkedesign.co.uk

Next up is Hilary Kerr, who has been my proofreader for a while now, and has a great eye for details I've missed, and some excellent editorial suggestions, as well as lots of greatly appreciated encouragement, too.

And my wonderful beta reading team, who give up their time to read the earliest versions of my books for absolutely nothing. That already tells you a lot about them! In no particular order, I owe a huge amount of thanks to: Marilynn Wrigley, Rebecca Leech, Ros Osborn, Kate Jenkins, Sandra Francis, Amanda Tudor, Ginnie Ebbrell, Tracey Shaw, Alison Lassey, Sheila Setter, Jean Crowe, Mandy Chowney-Andrews, and Nelly Harper. Both Marilynn and Nelly are also authors, and I'd recommend you look up their books.

I would also like to thank everyone who takes the time to comment on my Facebook posts, and send me messages, as your lovely remarks and encouragement really mean a great deal to me. It's heartening as a writer to know that your books mean something to other people.

At the time when covid really had us trapped – or 'safe' – at home, I remember thinking I would never want to write about it. That it was already real enough, and people often look to books to escape. But now, the situation is being played down, and I started to think we were at risk of forgetting just what we have all lived through. It's been a very, very strange couple of years. And without wishing to be a misery, we are not out of the woods yet. Even so, I found that those first early terrifying days were beginning to fade in my memory, and I really wanted to write it all down. But I didn't want it to be a thoroughly miserable story I was telling, so the Coming Back to Cornwall series seemed the perfect place to do this – a safe space.

For my family, as many of you know, covid struck the world just at the time my mum had received a diagnosis of uncurable cancer. Her treatment (chemotherapy) began at the same time as the first lockdown in the UK, and when she developed sepsis as a result, we were unable to go with her or visit her in hospital. She was released to a hospice, and we discovered then that she actually had covid herself. Ironically, it seemed to barely touch her, but it meant we were isolated from her again. And she had to try and recuperate in a strange place, with people she didn't know who were all dressed in full-on PPE. She rallied and came home, before deteriorating again. Covid affected us hugely, and Mum's funeral was limited to thirteen mourners, spaced two metres apart, and streamed live for those at home to see. There is no way to play down how deeply difficult that was.

As I have been working on *Time and Tide*, my dad and my brothers and I have been arranging a celebration of Mum's life, where we can get together with the people we would have liked to come to the funeral. And I also finally caught covid myself, at the time I was writing a book about it – which is probably poetic justice! It hit me hard for a couple of days, but gave me some great firsthand experience to lend some authenticity to the book.

I have set the release date for this book for two days after Mum's celebration. So by the time you read this, I hope that all will have gone according to plan, and I hope Mum would have approved of me mentioning her like this. It's not a plea for sympathy – it's just the fact that my family is just one of I don't know how many, whose lives have been affected by covid, sometimes in unseen and unimaginable ways. It is something which should not be underestimated, and should certainly not be forgotten. But just as Mum wanted a celebration for us all at a time that we could have one, I wanted a celebration in my book, for everyone, because we have all been affected, these last two years, in one way or another, and it's hard sometimes to remember to stop and be glad for the good things in life.

The first eight Coming Back to Cornwall books:

The Connections series: a group of stories whose protagonists' lives are inescapably interwoven, in the Cornish town they call home.

What dark secrets could a harmless old lady possibly know? Elise Morgan is nearly ninety years old. She loves her family, the sea, and night-time walks. She hates gossip, and bullies, and being called 'sweet', or treated like she's stupid, or boring (and sometimes like she's deaf), just because she has lived a long time.

Elise was sent to an all-girls' school, which was evacuated to Cornwall in the Second World War. She never left the county.

She is an orphan, a mother, a grandmother, and a widow. Since her children moved away and her best friend died, life has seemed increasingly empty.

These days, she spends a lot of time sitting at her window, looking out at the world, as if nothing ever happens, and nothing ever has. To passers-by, she might seem just an old lady, but of course there is no such thing. There was once a time when she lived a lot... and there are things she has never forgotten...

Maggie Cavendish is a single mum to Stevie, who has never known her dad, and that's how Maggie wants it to stay. Coming from a steady, stable family home herself, Maggie's world changed irrevocably when her father died, and she discovered something about him that she has never mentioned to her mum, or her twin sister.

Deemed 'the clever one' at school, expectations were set for Maggie from the outset, but what should have been a blessing often seemed exactly the opposite, particularly pitted against her popular and pretty sister Julia, and their best friend, Stacey. It's a surprise to everyone when Maggie discovers she is pregnant.

After years of living with her mum and her daughter, circumstances force Maggie to make a change, starting afresh in a small town on the coast. As Stevie settles in at school, Maggie finds voluntary work at the local seniors' club, and befriends eighty-something Elise. As other parts of her life begin to click into place — an exciting new job, and possibly a new relationship — she rediscovers her sense of self-esteem, and begins to regret not being more honest: with Elise; with her mum, sister and daughter; and with herself.

Also by Katharine E. Smith

Writing the Town Read - Katharine's first novel.

"I seriously couldn't put it down and would recommend it to anyone to doesn't like chick lit, but wants a great story."

Looking Past - a story of motherhood, and growing up without a mother.

"Despite the tough topic the book is full of love, friendships and humour. Katharine Smith cleverly balances emotional storylines with strong characters and witty dialogue, making this a surprisingly happy book to read."

Amongst Friends - a back-to-front tale of friendship and family, set in Bristol.

"An interesting, well written book, set in Bristol which is lovingly described, and with excellent characterisation. Very enjoyable."

Coming Back to Cornwall in audio

The whole Coming Back to Cornwall series is being made into audiobooks so you can now listen to the adventures of Alice, Julie and Sam while you drive, cook, clean, go to sleep… whatever, wherever! Watch out for more audiobooks in the series, coming soon…

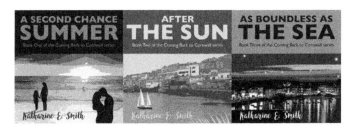

.